D0934372

ASPECTS

OF

ANXIETY

Second and Enlarged Edition

ATALANTA, BEAUTIFUL AND BELLIGERENT VIRGIN HUNTRESS OF GREEK mythology, symbolizes rejection of femininity. Born to a father who wished for a son, she scorns all lovers, slaying the centaurs and others who woo her. Reluctantly she gives her hand to Hippomenes who, challenged by her to a race, defeats her—succeeding only by dropping on the course three golden apples (given him by Aphrodite), which Atalanta stoops to pick up. *See* Chapter 13, *Anxiety and the Female Psyche.*

Library
I.U.P.
Indiana, PA

616,852
As63a2
C.2

Second and Enlarged Edition

ASPECTS

OF

ANXIETY

With a Preface by
C. H. HARDIN BRANCH, MD
PROFESSOR AND CHAIRMAN, DEPARTMENT OF PSYCHIATRY
UNIVERSITY OF UTAH COLLEGE OF MEDICINE, SALT LAKE CITY

J. B. LIPPINCOTT COMPANY
Philadelphia & Toronto

Library
I.U.P.
Indiana, Pa.

616.852   As63a2
c.2

THE FURIES. IN GREEK MYTHOLOGY, SNAKY-HAIRED GODDESSES, armed with torches and whips, pursued the guilty offender who had violated the laws of piety and hospitality or was guilty of perjury or homicide—inflicting upon him madness and torment. Not so differently, modern psychiatric thought considers guilt and guilt feelings not only as manifestations in numerous neurotic conditions but also as their frequent and potent instigator. *See* Chapter 16, *Anxiety and Guilt.*

Copyright © 1965, 1968 by J. B. LIPPINCOTT COMPANY

This book is fully protected by copyright and, with the exception of brief abstracts for review, no part of it may be reproduced in any form without the written permission of the publisher.

Distributed in Great Britain by
Pitman Medical Publishing Company, Limited, London
Library of Congress Catalog Card No. 68-27538
PRINTED IN THE UNITED STATES OF AMERICA
SP-B

PREFACE *to Second and Enlarged Edition*

THIS ENLARGED edition has considerably expanded the material on anxiety previously presented to internists and other practitioners of medicine. The new material should add considerably to the usefulness of the book to physicians everywhere.

Although anxiety would seem at first glance to be a problem primarily visible in the psychiatrist's office, actually internists and others are usually the first physicians to see psychiatric problems. The result has been an increased interest in improving the psychiatric orientation of all physicians and the presentation of a wide range of educational programs at both the undergraduate and the postgraduate levels.

The changing economics of medical practice makes it even more important for the patient to have a "primary physician" to whom he can turn for all his medical problems, no matter what that physician's specialty may be. This concept is probably more useful than the traditional one of "the family physician," because what is developing now is a physician whose help the patient routinely seeks, recognizing that his specialty may be obstetrics, orthopedics, or internal medicine, but that his knowledge of the patient's total needs would be sufficient to enable him either to handle the problem or to make adequate referral to an individual to whom he provides the introduction.

The addition of several chapters to this book broadens its usefulness to physicians. "Anxiety and Pain," for example, emphasizes the difference between pain and suffering and the relationship of both to anxiety, a matter of tremendous importance to the physician attempting to evaluate the total situation relating to his patient's care.

It has been pointed out that patients, especially in the social levels now very much a part of general medical practice—that is, those below middle class—come to their "primary physicians" with a variety of complaints, some frankly somatic. While many of these patients will eventually require attention to the psy-

5

chological aspects of their problem, it is necessary that the physician be able to evaluate the total picture, viewing the problem through the eyes of the patient who sees his symptoms as primarily somatic.

It is essential, therefore, that physicians be alert to the meaning of the symptoms of which their patients complain. When anxiety is a hidden part of the problem, the physician must recognize the protean nature of the symptom and the somatic conditions with which it is associated.

Encompassing these considerations in the initial work-up of the patient greatly facilitates subsequent referral or treatment of the psychiatric aspects of the problem. Ignoring these considerations may require the primary physician to backtrack from a predominantly somatic approach to the problem at the cost of some embarrassment to himself and his patient.

Furthermore, the changing economic picture is also reflected in various difficulties having to do with the masculine role in our culture and the consequent special anxieties of the male, and this is considered in a new chapter on "Anxiety As a Reaction to Family Illness" and in the discussion on terminal illnesses as they affect the family constellation, particularly important and valuable. An additional new inclusion is the whole question of anxiety as it relates to economic security.

It is for the purpose of bringing these matters to the attention of the primary physicians that these chapters have been collated by Roche Laboratories into a single volume. Every attempt has been made to present this material factually and practically, and the practicing physician should find in these pages considerable help, both in recognizing the various facets of anxiety and its physiological concomitants, and in attempting to chart the best therapeutic course for the patients for whom he is responsible.

C. H. HARDIN BRANCH, MD
Head, Department of Psychiatry
University of Utah Medical Center
Past-President, American Psychiatric Association

CONTENTS

FIGHT OR FLIGHT

The Nature and Meaning of Anxiety

A NXIETY has been defined in various ways: as, for instance, "a specific unpleasurable state of tension which indicates the presence of some danger to the organism," [1] or as "the apprehensive tension or uneasiness which stems from the anticipation of imminent danger, in which the source is largely unknown or unrecognized." [2] However it may be described, the unpleasantness of anxiety is invariably stressed. It is this aspect, perhaps more than any other, that makes anxiety so important a force in human existence. Subjectively uncomfortable and painful, anxiety not only warns the individual that "something is wrong", but generally goads him into seeking out the source of danger so that it can be eliminated. In moderate degree, anxiety can be termed a constructive force, serving to increase alertness and effort.

THE UNPLEASANT EMOTION

The role of anxiety is particularly prominent in individual character formation and personality development. [2] The uneasiness and apprehension aroused by the disapproval of parents, for instance, often bring about constructive changes in a child's behavior. In both children and adults, levels of anxiety within the individual's capacity to cope with it are conducive to learning and to growth. In addition, anxiety is frequently a strong motivating force in decision-making, its unpleasantness pushing the individual toward the resolution of some inhibiting impasse caused by internal conflicts. [3]

As with any stimulus, however, a massive "dose" can defeat its own purpose by causing overreaction or complete paralysis. In excess, anxiety can cause disjunctive and pathologic behavior. It is, in fact, probably at the root of most neurotic and nonorganic psychotic illness. To allay the highly unpleasant emotion of anxiety, man unconsciously employs various mechanisms. These lead to the formation of symptoms, some of them unhealthful—such as the phobias, somatic conversions and dissociative reactions. Thus, "the

9

symptoms which develop psychogenetically in emotional illness are ultimately to be considered as the result of defensive efforts against anxiety." [2] Equally important, since anxiety is not simply a subjective emotion but is accompanied by bodily changes, excessive anxiety often produces somatic consequences as well.

THE BODY'S RESPONSE TO ANXIETY

Clinically, the body's response to intense anxiety and to fear is almost identical. Palpitation, tachycardia, sweating, pallor, urinary frequency, vertigo, headache, chest pain, syncope, anorexia, nausea, abdominal cramps, tremors, weakness, sleeplessness—all (in different degrees and in various individually occurring combinations) may be present in the person caught up in a life-threatening situation.[4] And they are just as likely to be present in the individual who, to the observer at least, faces no "real" danger but simply has the feeling that "something is wrong, something terrible is going to happen."

The similarity of symptoms is hardly surprising. Anxiety, like fear and anger, arises in response to danger or threat. In 1916, Cannon [5] first spotlighted the biologic significance of these intense emotions: "Fear has become associated with the instinct to run, to escape, and anger or aggressive feeling with the instinct to attack. These are fundamental emotions and instincts which have resulted from the experience of multitudes of generations in the fierce struggle for existence and which have their values in that struggle."

Describing the bodily changes that accompany these emotions, Cannon emphasized that the physiologic responses to emotional excitement are designed to prepare the organism for emergency action—"fight or flight"—at the expense of digestion and other visceral functions. When the cortex of the brain perceives a threat, he noted, it sends a stimulus down the sympathetic branch of the autonomic nervous system to the adrenal glands. Under the influence of epinephrine, respiration deepens, the heart beats more rapidly, the arterial pressure rises; blood is shifted away from the stomach and intestines to the heart, central nervous system and the muscles; processes in the alimentary canal are inhibited; glycogenolysis is accelerated and the blood glucose level increased; the spleen contracts and discharges its store of corpuscles. All of these physiologic changes—particularly the increased respiration, the redistributed blood flowing at higher pressure, and the increased number of red corpuscles set free by the spleen, which provide for essential oxygen and for riddance of acid waste—serve to render the body more effective in the violent display of energy that response to danger may demand.

While Cannon's observations continue to serve as focal points for present thinking, evidence increases that the "physiology of emotions" involves the organism much more extensively and in a far more complex manner than originally recognized. For instance, although Cannon and his collaborators considered the sympathetic nervous system the structure principally concerned with adjustment to stress, later workers found that the parasympathetic system was also prominently involved—thus explaining why such effects as increased frequency of urination, emptying of the rectum, slowing of the heart rate and lowered blood pressure may also be part of the anxiety syndrome.[6] Selye, who described his General Adaptation Syndrome in 1936, focused attention on the vital role of the pituitary-adrenocortic axis in the body's response to stress.[7] Many of the details of the complex interrelationship between emotional, visceral and somatic reactions have yet to be fully established. A key structure, certainly, would be the hypothalamus, known to coordinate the muscular and visceral functions especially essential in coping with emergency situations.[8] The rhinencephalon, too, plays an important role in integrating emotional and visceral activity, and recent studies suggest the hypothalamus and rhinencephalon may be largely responsible for the secondary somatic manifestations of anxiety.[9]

THE RETICULAR ACTIVATING SYSTEM

Many investigators feel that the central neurophysiologic processes underlying anxiety may be found in the reticular activating system. Stimulation of this system—which comprises both the midbrain reticular formation and the diffuse thalamocortical projections—makes for alertness or arousal both in behavior and in the EEG; depression of this system leads to various degrees of relaxation or sleepiness. In addition, stimulation of this system not only alerts the organism but also probably provides an "emotional cloak" to incoming sensory impressions. An important reason for the diverse effects achieved by various psychopharmacologic agents is that they differ in their intensity of action on each of the various subcortical structures most concerned with emotions—the midbrain reticular formation, the hypothalamus, and the components of the rhinencephalon.[8]

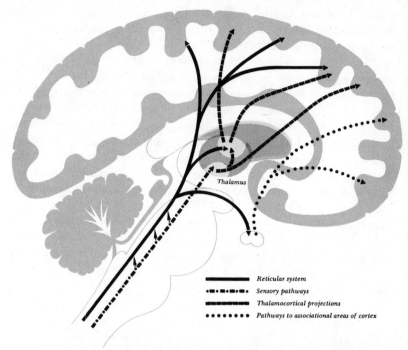

Reticular system
Sensory pathways
Thalamocortical projections
Pathways to associational areas of cortex

Fig. 1. The reticular activating system. This system parallels the classical sensory pathways. Impulses that ascend the sensory tract to the cortex bring discriminatory awareness of a stimulus. At the same time, however, the activating system, which receives collaterals from the sensory pathways, alerts the cortex and is probably also responsible for an emotional reaction to the stimulus.

CHRONIC MOBILIZATION

During temporary states of emergency or stress, the human organism has little trouble maintaining its equilibrium throughout its all-out mobilization of bodily resources. Although tensions are built up, these can usually be discharged, if not into "fight or flight," at least into physical activity of one kind or another. However, while fear and anxiety are sometimes used interchangeably, the two emotions have an essential difference that can have far-reaching clinical importance. Fear, an emotional response to a consciously recognized and usually external threat or danger, generally tends to be short-lived; when the danger passes, the emotion and its physiologic manifestations tend to fade away. Anxiety, on the other hand, the emotional response to a danger usually internal and not readily recognized, is not likely to be quickly dispelled. Anxiety can thus persist indefinitely, and Wolff points out that ". . . man, feeling threatened, may use for long-term purposes devices designed for short-term needs. They are not designed to be used as lifelong patterns and when so utilized may damage structures they were designed to protect." [10]

States of chronic anxiety have been found, therefore, to have a number of effects on the body. One of the most detailed listings of the physical manifestations of anxiety was presented by D. Ewen Cameron in his paper, "Observations on the Patterns of Anxiety." [11] Cameron found that his tense and anxious patients tended to fall into three groups: those in whom the skeletal musculature was mainly involved, those in whom the smooth musculature reacted most prominently (generally with either gastrointestinal or cardiovascular symptoms), and those in whom skeletal and smooth musculature appeared equally involved.

Skeletal muscle patterns were the most common. The fundamental basis of somatic complaints of the patients in this group was an increase in the skeletal muscle tonus. Simple increase in muscular tension resulted in increased tendon reflexes, occasional transitory knee and ankle clonus, and both external and internal tremor. Increased energy expenditure, brought about by prolonged muscle tonus, led to such symptoms as generalized fatigue and weakness. More complex derivatives of muscle tension included clumsiness of the hands and feet, jerking of limbs before going to sleep, facial tics, tightening of the throat, unsteadiness of the voice, "weaving," a feeling of unsteadiness and, in exceptional cases, inability to move at all during periods of tension. The next most common physical manifestations of anxiety were cardiovascular. The patients in this group had such symptoms as precordial pressure and pain, palpitation, throbbing sensations, sensations of heat, constriction of the veins, fast pulse and high blood pressure. Interestingly enough, fears about losing one's mind or of sudden death seemed restricted to those patients showing the cardiovascular response to anxiety. The third largest group of patients had predominantly gastrointestinal complaints and suffered from nausea, borborygmus, epigastric sensations, feelings of "emptiness," heartburn, cramps and bad taste in the mouth.

Individual patients appeared to react characteristically to anxiety: "The pattern dominant during the period of a patient's life when he was showing a normal anxiety reaction tends to remain dominant when his anxiety reaches abnormal levels of intensity." [11] Thus, the person who once reacted to sudden fright with a rapidly beating heart and precordial pressure was the one most likely, during anxiety states, to visit the physician because of "cardiac" symptoms. The person who responded to dangerous situations with trembling voice, hands and knees was the one most likely, when anxiety became pathologically intensified, to complain of tremor, muscle aches and feelings of stiffness.

EMOTIONAL "FIGHT OR FLIGHT"

Even a brief introduction to this complex problem clearly indicates that states of chronic anxiety can have important physical and emotional repercussions. Certainly continuous increased activity of the autonomic nervous system can be a potent aggravating and even causative factor in many illnesses. And—as has been pointed out above—just as the body mobilizes for possible emergency action, the mind automatically moves either to escape or to eliminate what has been termed a "major source of human discomfort." [2] This symbolic "fight or flight" reaction to the "pain" of anxiety results in the use of mental mechanisms (repression, conversion, denial, projection) or in the formation of character defensive traits. In certain cases, the reaction may lead to the development of clinical psychoneuroses and psychoses. Subsequent chapters in *Aspects of Anxiety* will explore more fully the role of anxiety in man's physical and emotional life.

CHAPTER 1 BIBLIOGRAPHY

1. Weiss, E., and English, O. S.: Psychosomatic Medicine, Philadelphia, Saunders, 1957.
2. Laughlin, H. P.: The Neuroses in Clinical Practice, Philadelphia, Saunders, 1956.
3. Jenkins, R. L.: The Medical Significance of Anxiety, Washington (DC), The Biological Science Foundation Ltd., 1955.
4. Aldrich, C. K.: Psychiatry for the Family Physician, New York, McGraw-Hill, 1955.
5. Cannon, W. B.: The Wisdom of the Human Body, New York, Norton, rev ed, 1939.
6. Grinker, R. R.: Psychosom Med *1*:19, 1939.
7. Selye, H.: The Stress of Life, New York, McGraw-Hill, 1956.
8. Himwich, H. E.: *in* Uhr, L., and Miller, J. G., eds.: Drugs and Behavior, New York, Wiley, 1960, pp. 41 ff.
9. Kolb, L. C.: J Chron Dis *9*:199, 1959.
10. Wolff, H. G.: A Res Nerv & Ment Dis Proc, 1949, *29*:1059, 1950.
11. Cameron, D. E.: Amer J Psychiat *101*:36, 1944.

ANXIETY — A KEY TO PERSONALITY

A LTHOUGH ANXIETY has hundreds of causes in contemporary life, many consider its true cornerstone the constant clash between man's instinctual drives and society's frustrating demands.[1, 2] The principal function of society has always been, in effect, to block the fulfillment of many of man's natural instincts. By the time he is ready for school, even the child has learned that a number of his impulses must be controlled, modified or sublimated if he is to be approved by his family and accepted by his companions—his community. But no matter how civilized the individual may eventually become, he never stops fighting a constant, albeit often subconscious, battle between, on the one hand, his natural desires—e.g., possession, vengeance, love or sex—and, on the other, the social and personal standards of morality and behavior that he has been taught.

The Internal Censor

According to most psychiatrists, then, the major source of man's anxiety is his conscience (or superego), an internal censor that starts developing quite early in life, largely in response to the real or assumed attitudes of the persons close to a child. As the child grows up, he either accepts and internalizes the standards of these persons, or rejects some of them and substitutes others in their place. He eventually acquires a system of what he "knows" to be right-and-wrong. When this internal censor clashes with the individual's unconscious desires and impulses, his personality is, in a sense, divided—and a feeling of apprehension, of tension or inner restlessness, occurs.[2]

Of course, anxiety has other sources. Although the conscience takes over much of the approval-disapproval function formerly held by parents, teachers and other influential adults, it can never eliminate the human being's very real need to be approved by others. Next to his built-in censor, the individual's second most important source of anxiety is undoubtedly the disapproval, or fear of disapproval, of other people—and particularly of those persons most important in an adult's life, such as his family, close friends, and employers.[1] The influence of this source of anxiety varies with each individual, some people being less able than others to lose their early strong dependency needs. In addition, quite real threats to self-preservation crop up in everyone's life. "Normal" anxiety is experienced in the face of such realities as illness, old age and death. Some feeling of apprehension is probably always present whenever an individual moves from a sheltered, certain and tested situation to a new and unknown one. And whenever genuine values—love, freedom, equality, self-respect—are threatened, a state of anxiety is inevitable.[3]

Man's Attempts to Alleviate Anxiety

Whatever its source, anxiety is so unpleasant an emotion that the instinctive tendency is to eliminate it as swiftly as possible or at least to remove it from conscious awareness. Therefore, a variety of complex mental mechanisms operate on an automatic, round-the-clock nonconscious basis to "fight or flee" anxiety and to resolve the emotional conflict that may have caused it (see THE MENTAL MECHANISMS OF EGO DEFENSE). The most commonly used of these mechanisms is repression. Through repression, disturbing impulses and thoughts are conveniently excluded from the mind and "pushed down" into the unconscious. Experiences that involve guilt, shame, or the lowering of self-esteem—all ideas or memories that might arouse painful anxiety—are especially apt to be repressed. But though not subject to conscious recall, repressed material continues to retain much dynamic drive. In the effort to reinforce repression and prevent its breakthrough into the conscious mind, one or more other mental mechanisms may be called into play, sometimes resulting in an "indirect" release of the repressed emotion.

As an example, Laughlin [1] describes a 28-year-old school teacher who, for no apparent reason, frequently became enraged with her principal, an older woman. Investigation revealed that the teacher's hostility was actually directed toward her own unpleasant mother. Because this emotion was so intolerable, the young teacher not only repressed it but, in order to reinforce the repression, released the negative feelings toward what was to her a more acceptable substi-

THE MENTAL MECHANISMS OF EGO DEFENSE: A SELECTIVE GLOSSARY [1]

These mechanisms are vital mental processes, operating outside and beyond conscious awareness, through which the individual attempts to relieve emotional tension, anxiety and conflict. In almost all cases, two or more mental mechanisms operate concurrently.

COMPENSATION. The unconscious effort to make up for real or fancied deficiencies. A kind of "characterologic hypertrophy" can result from overcompensation.

DENIAL. One of the simplest and most primitive ego defenses, through which consciously intolerable material is disowned by the unconscious denial of its existence. Thus, through denial the clearly terminal case can appear "not to see" all evidence of approaching death.

DISPLACEMENT. An unconscious process—and the one largely responsible for the development of phobic reactions—by which an emotional feeling is transferred from its actual object (usually an internal one) to a substitute and external one.

DISSOCIATION. A mechanism by which the emotional significance and affect are separated and detached from an idea, situation or object. Thus, the use of dissociation allows relatives to postpone grief, in effect, while they "calmly" make funeral arrangements for a loved one.

IDENTIFICATION. The unconscious process by which an individual endeavors to make himself like another, perhaps by transferring to himself the thoughts, mannerisms, tastes or behavior of the second person.

INTERNALIZATION. The process by which external attributes, attitudes or standards are taken within oneself, i.e., internalized.

PROJECTION. A mechanism whereby consciously disowned aspects of the self are rejected and thrown outward to become imputed to others. Through the operation of this widespread process, an individual can attribute his own intolerable wishes, emotional feelings or motivations to other persons.

RATIONALIZATION. An unconscious process by which the ego justifies or attempts to make otherwise unacceptable impulses, feelings, behavior and motives into consciously tolerable and acceptable ones.

REACTION FORMATION. A process by which needs, complexes, attitudes and motives are developed in large areas of the personality which are the *reverse* of those consciously repudiated. Thus, a person's outward attitude of overconcern may have been developed to hide inner feelings of hostility.

REGRESSION. The term employed to describe the psychic process of returning, in a more or less symbolic fashion, to an earlier and subjectively more satisfactory level of adjustment.

REPRESSION. The most widely used mechanism, an involuntary and automatic relegation of unbearable ideas and impulses into the unconscious, whence they are not ordinarily subject to voluntary conscious recall.

RESTITUTION. The attempt to assuage unconscious guilt feelings by making some kind of reparation.

SUBLIMATION. A mental mechanism through which consciously unacceptable instinctual drives are diverted into personally and socially acceptable channels.

SUBSTITUTION. An unconscious process by which an unacceptable goal, emotion, or object is replaced by one more acceptable.

SYMBOLIZATION. A widely used process by which an object, usually external, becomes the disguised outward representation for another internal and hidden object or idea.

UNDOING. One of the more primitive mechanisms, in which a prior act, thought or impulse is erased or undone. In compulsive reactions such as hand-washing, for instance, a symbolic act often serves as a sort of magic ritual by which an individual *undoes* or annuls the possible effect of his unrecognized impulses.

tute—the principal. Even when developed in somewhat exaggerated fashion, mental mechanisms are not necessarily disruptive. A too-protective mother, for instance, may be suspected of using an excessive show of concern to mask from herself an unconscious hostility toward her child—but, in all probability, the woman may still be a reasonably happy and efficient individual.

The use of some mental mechanisms as defenses against anxiety appears to be essential for all human beings if they are to retain emotional stability. As Saul wrote: "There is no one so free of repressions, so entirely at one with his conscience and standards, that he has no inner anxieties whatever; few persons, if any, do not have some irrational fears. . . ." [4] The nature and number of the defenses each person habitually uses often strongly influence his personality pattern. The use of too many defenses, for instance, usually results in a more constricted, rigid type of personality. If mental mechanisms become highly exaggerated or disorganized (and as anxiety increases, defenses against it tend to become less efficient and less rational), they result in neurotic or even psychotic personalities.[2]

The Emotionally Crippled

Thus while defenses against anxiety may contribute to the individual's emotional equilibrium, when overused or used unsuccessfully they are responsible for many of the emotional symptoms that can "cripple" an individual as effectively as physical disease.

For instance, the development of an obsessive-compulsive neurosis, greatly simplified, might evolve as follows: [5] a child, made anxious because of strong negative feelings toward his parents, attempts to deal with this anxiety by repressing all trace of hostility. But repression alone is not enough. To reinforce repression, the child displaces his hostility to an activity that irritates his parents (and is therefore symbolically hostile), such as soiling. His impulse to dirty himself and others is then supercharged; and to counteract this second uncomfortable impulse, the child becomes continually preoccupied with cleanliness. In time, an obsessive-compulsive reaction forms. How incapacitating this can be is illustrated by Aldrich's patient who was so obsessed with cleanliness that she spent the entire day in the bathroom, washing and re-washing her hands.[5] "Crippling" phobias, somatic conversions and a host of other emotional ills also stem from the personality's misguided efforts to deal with excessive anxiety.

When anxiety succeeds in breaking through the defenses against it, it can be equally handicapping, particularly when it persists. As Laughlin points out, an individual who experiences an anxiety attack in a subway tends to associate his acute discomfort with the subway itself and tries to avoid riding in one from then on. If subsequent attacks occur in other situations, these are avoided as well. Thus, the person gradually restricts more and more of his activities as he encounters more places, experiences and situations that he feels must be avoided. Because of the restrictive effect of anxiety, probably every physician has at least one patient who cannot come in for treatment because he (or she) is afraid to ride buses, is afraid to walk the streets alone, is afraid even to leave the house.[1]

Yet while anxiety is a central problem in many emotional and physical ills, it may be well to remember that it is also "a prime factor in human behavior, in the development of personality, and in the formation of the individual character defenses or traits."[1]

CHAPTER 2 BIBLIOGRAPHY

1. Laughlin, H. P.: The Neuroses in Clinical Practice, Philadelphia, Saunders, 1956, p. 33, *passim.*
2. Noyes, A. P.: Modern Clinical Psychiatry, Philadelphia, Saunders, 1953.
3. Portnoy, I.: *in* Arietti, S., ed.: American Handbook of Psychiatry, vol 1, New York, Basic, 1959.
4. Saul, L. J.: Amer J Psychiat *106:*547, 1950.
5. Aldrich, C. K.: Psychiatry for the Family Physician, New York, McGraw-Hill, 1955.

ANXIETY AND THE HEART

━━

C ORONARY ARTERY DISEASE is, in many respects, the prosperous man's illness. Relatively uncommon among the hungry and underfed, its chief victims appear to be those "fortunate" individuals who can afford to overeat and underexercise. It is not surprising then, that in well-fed America, where the average diet is also exceptionally rich in animal fat, the cardiovascular disease death rate is the highest in the world. However, no simple cause-and-effect relationship exists between high-fat diets and atherosclerosis. Hereditary influences are undoubtedly important. Age and sex play roles, with men over forty by far the most likely candidates for coronary artery diseases in this country. It has been suggested, though, that sex differences may be less important than "the masculine love for rich food, alcohol and tobacco." [1]

Stress as "Catalyst"

In a society like ours, much of the lethal effect of a high-fat diet coupled with insufficient exercise often seems dependent on the "catalytic" influence of stressful living. Short-lived anxiety and tension alone probably have little effect on the healthy heart and arteries. But in those already predisposed to coronary troubles—because of overweight, hypertension or hypercholesterolemia—anxiety and tension appear to compound this susceptibility more than any other factors.[2] For example, in studies conducted in a group of 100 coronary patients under 40 years of age, it was found that prolonged emotional strain associated with job responsibility preceded a coronary occlusion in 91% of cases. In a control group of patients with other diseases, only 20% had been under similar strain. Job-related emotional stress also appeared to be far more significant in the etiology of coronary disease, at least in these younger adults, than heredity, the quantity of fat ingested daily, or other factors studied (see Table 1).[3]

That the coronary disease patient often has a demanding job—and

TABLE 1. *% incidence of various factors in subjects [3] with coronary disease and control group* *

GROUP	CORONARY DISEASE	CONTROL	RATIO
Heredity (positive)	67	40	1.7 : 1
High-fat diet	53	20	2.7 : 1
Emotional stress (occup.)	91	20	4.6 : 1
Tobacco †	70	35	2 : 1
Lack of exercise	42	40	1 : 1
Obesity	26	20	1.3 : 1

* 100 subjects in each group   † 30 cigarets or more per day

one associated with constant strain—has been frequently noted. The amount of responsibility attached to the position appears more important than the actual occupation. Gertler and White, for instance, found that coronary disease in their young adult patients was not confined to any one occupational class but that its incidence was relatively higher in managerial and executive positions.[4] Men in such positions not only are subjected to fairly continuous emotional stress, but often have achieved their responsible posts through sustained, unflagging effort. Thus, as several studies have suggested, the intensity with which certain individuals react to daily situations may be a factor in their higher incidence of coronary disease. Friedman and Rosenman found that, in a group of men whose behavior was characterized by ambition, competitive drive and constant preoccupation with "deadlines," clinical coronary artery disease was seven times more frequent than in a comparable group whose members were distinctly more relaxed in their daily pursuits.[5]

If "emotional exertion" apparently increases an individual's susceptibility to coronary disease, physical exertion seems to decrease it; by and large, men in physically active jobs—whatever their temperament—tend to have a lower incidence of coronary heart disease in middle age than men in physically inactive jobs.[6] By a clinically unfortunate coincidence, however, occupations that generate the most emotional tension often demand the least physically. Therefore, while opinions may differ about which, if any, occupations contribute most to the development of coronary disease, "One has the definite impression," Paul White has observed, "that it is distinctly less common in the lean laborer or farmer."[7]

Stress, Strain and Cardiac Dynamics

The exact mechanism by which prolonged emotional strain contributes to clinical coronary artery disease has not been established;

there are various possibilities. For one, emotional stress is known to increase circulatory requirements.[8-10] The effects are brought about through impulses playing on the cardiac and vasomotor centers in the medulla. Liberation of epinephrine into the blood stream may also be a factor; in the majority of persons, anxiety has an effect on the circulation similar to that produced by small doses of epinephrine.[11] Because anxiety may significantly increase the amount of work required of the heart, anxiety-induced arrhythmias —including paroxysmal tachycardia, premature systoles, atrial fibrillation, and even paroxysmal ventricular tachycardia—may occur in individuals who have no other detectable evidence of heart disease. That disorders of cardiac rhythm can be precipitated by "threatening" situations is clearly illustrated by data obtained from students before examination and 24 hours later (see Fig. 2).[12]

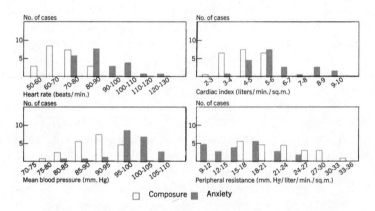

Fig. 2. Effect of anxiety on various circulatory values.[9]

Electrocardiographic studies have also repeatedly demonstrated that the heart is a sensitive indicator of the physiologic state accompanying anxiety and stress.[13] In the majority of these studies, the following changes were correlated with a state of emotional tension: 1. increased P wave amplitude; 2. depression, inversion or distortion of the T wave; 3. ST segment deviation. These changes are associated with increased sympathetic tone, although some reports [13] also observed parasympathetic influences. Particularly significant are tracings obtained from patients exercised during a period of emotional stress: marked ST-T changes were present, while the same exercise on a day of emotional relaxation produced less change or none at all.[15] And during states of emotional tension, circulation was found to recover slowly and inefficiently from the effects of exercise, thus prolonging the strain on the heart.[16]

Suggested Mechanisms of Intimal Damage

In addition to all these changes in circulatory dynamics, important metabolic alterations also accompany periods of physical and emotional stress. Lipid-regulating mechanisms seem to be particularly responsive to emotional upheaval. During threatening situations, blood viscosity and shortening of clotting times also increase: clotting times of the blood were accelerated in medical students on the morning of their final examination,[17] for instance (Fig. 3), and in

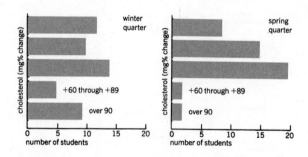

Fig. 3. Changes in serum cholesterols during final medical school examinations.[20]

accountants as the income tax deadline neared.[18] Although clearly of some advantage during actual emergencies (where presumably they would minimize blood loss), these protective mechanisms could be harmful if invoked too constantly. A fairly permanent circulatory state of "emergency" could possibly mean that blood with increased coagulability and decreased fluidity might slow sufficiently in passing through narrowed coronary or cerebral arteries to produce thrombosis.[2]

Epinephrine and norepinephrine have been demonstrated to be potentially injurious to vascular tissue. An excess of their endogenous formation and release, by damaging the intima, may increase its lipid receptiveness. At any rate, animal experiments have indicated that the depositing of cholesterol in the intima appears to be accelerated and intensified by epinephrine. In addition, striking elevations in cholesterol levels are sometimes seen during stressful situations, indicating that nonesterified fatty acids from body tissues may also be mobilized during stress in order to "provide metabolic substrate for the aroused organism" (see Fig. 3).[2,19] This mobilization would certainly increase the possibility of abnormal lipid

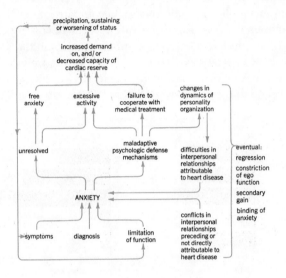

Fig. 4. Feedback cycles of anxiety. In cardiac disease they are essentially operative in 2 ways: (a) untoward effects of anxiety upon the tenuous circulatory balance, (b) behavior problems stemming from maladaptive ego defense against anxiety.[23]

depositions, particularly in an organism already oversupplied with circulating fat molecules because of impaired lipid metabolism or high-fat diet. Overactivity of the sympathoadrenal system and an excess amount of epinephrine and norepinephrine may also exert injurious influences on myocardial oxygen economy and myocardial mechanical efficiency. Catecholamines, if not sufficiently counteracted by vagal acetylcholine, according to W. Raab,[2] impair myocardial efficiency, waste oxygen in a disproportionate fashion and are thus capable of inducing severe, potentially necrotizing myocardial hypoxia,[21] particularly in a heart which already has a diminished blood supply due to the presence of coronary atherosclerosis.

ibrary
.U.P.
ana, Pa.

616.852   A63a2
C. 2

Feedback Cycles of Cardiac Disease

The hypothesis that sustained emotional stress can cause coronary artery disease remains to be definitely proved. However, in the patient with existing structural heart disease and diminished cardiac reserve, emotional stress undoubtedly often produces or accentuates symptoms. Emotional factors, for instance, may help precipitate congestive heart failure in patients with diminished reserve, elevate arterial pressure enough to constitute a serious problem in the management of patients with essential hypertension, and frequently be implicated in the development of anginal pain (see Fig. 4).

Cardiac patients, like other patients with serious diseases, have good reason to be concerned about their ailment. When, however, they react to their illness with anxiety of a disproportionate or dangerous degree, the use of psychotropic therapy can often be helpful—both by "preventing symptoms through dampening emotional reactivity" [22] and by improving the patient's outlook on life.

CHAPTER 3 BIBLIOGRAPHY

1. Dock, I. W.: JAMA *170*:152, 1959.
2. Russek, H. I.: JAMA *171*:503, 1959.
3. Russek, H. I., and Zohman, B. L.: Amer J. Med Sci *235*:266, 1958.
4. Gertler, M. M., and White, P. D.: Coronary Heart Disease in Young Adults: Multidisciplinary Study, Cambridge, published for Commonwealth Fund, Harvard, 1954, p. 65.
5. Friedman, M., and Rosenman, R. H.: JAMA *169*:1286, 1959.
6. Morris, J. N., et al.: Lancet *2*:1111, 1953.
7. White, P. D.: Diseases of the Heart, ed 2, New York, Macmillan, 1937.
8. Wolff, G. A., Jr., and Wolff, H. G.: Psychosom Med *8*:293, 1946.
9. Hickam, J. B., et al.: J Clin Invest *207*:290, 1948.
10. Duncan, I. P., et al.: Geriatrics *6*:164, 1951.
11. Best, C. H., and Taylor, N. B.: The Physiological Basis of Medical Practice, ed 5, Baltimore, Williams & Wilkins, pp. 155 ff.
12. Wolf, S.: Mod Conc Cardiov Dis *29*:599, 1960.
13. Weiss, B.: Amer J Psychiat *113*:348, 1956.
14. Mainzer, F., and Krause, M.: Brit Heart J *2*:221, 1940.
15. Stevenson, I. P., et al.: Geriatrics *6*:164, 1951.
16. ————: J Clin Invest *28*:1534, 1949.
17. Dreyfuss, F., and Czaczekes, J. W.: Arch Intern Med (Chicago) *103*:708, 1959.
18. Friedman, M., Rosenman, R. H., Carroll, V.: Circulation *17*:852, 1958.
19. Bogdanoff, M. D., et al.: Psychophysiologic Studies of Fat Metabolism, 40th An'l Session American College of Physicians, Chicago, Apr 22, 1959.
20. Grundy, S. M., and Griffin, A. C.: Circulation *19*:496, 1959.
21. Raab, W.: Arch Intern Med (Chicago) *101*:194, 1958.
22. Cohen, I.: Angiology *13*:1, 1962.
23. Reiser, M. F., and Bakst, H.: in Arieti, S., ed.: American Handbook of Psychiatry, vol 1, New York, Basic, 1959, pp. 659 ff.

ANXIETY AND THE SKIN

T HE SKIN might logically be termed a "mirror" of man's emo-
     tions. Not only can the skin reflect sudden changes in mood and
feeling, but it often manages to do so in a vivid and unmistakable
fashion. When the individual is "white as a sheet," "hot under the
collar," or "covered with goose flesh," his state of mind is displayed
for the world to see. The commonest physiologic manifestations of
the skin—vasoconstriction, vasodilation, pilomotor activity and sweating—are regulated chiefly by the autonomic nervous system (see
Fig. 5) and are presumably part of man's over-all "fight or flight"
reaction to stress situations. Such emotional expressions as blushing,
pallor and sweating have been called "a kind of atavistic cutaneous
sign language by which inhibited instincts are betrayed." [1]

TABLE 2. *107 active members of the American Dermatological Association reply
to the first 2 items of a questionnaire. Q 1: Do you believe that psychogenic
factors are important in the development of any dermatologic condition? Yes:
106, No: 1. Q 2: Do you believe that psychogenic factors are important in the
development of the following? See below:*

DISORDER	YES	QUESTIONABLE	NO	UNANSWERED
Atopic dermatitis	82	2	3	20
Neurodermatitis	84	2	0	21
Neurotic excoriations	105	0	0	2
Sometimes	1	0	0	0
Other factitial dermatoses	99	2	0	6
Trichotillomania	98	1	1	7
Alopecia areata	53	15	5	34
Sometimes	1	0	0	0
Lichen planus	54	17	6	30
Occasionally	4	0	0	0

Role of Emotional Stress

Clinically, skin diseases may be due largely to genetic faults, to
chemical and physical effects, to the influence of drugs or bacteria

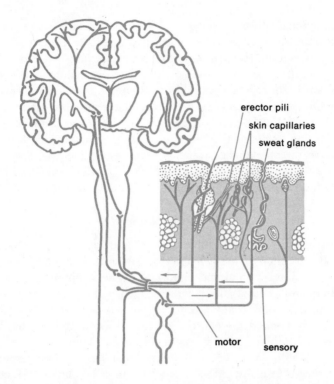

erector pili

skin capillaries

sweat glands

motor

sensory

Fig. 5. In the skin, the spinal nerves provide the sensory pathway, while autonomic fibers supply the motor system. In the latter, cholinergic fibers activate the secretory cells of the eccrine sweat gland; adrenergic fibers activate the myoepithelium of both sweat glands and the smooth muscle of the arteriole and erector pili. Afferent sensory nerves conduct impulses giving rise to sensations of pruritus, pain, touch and temperature. By all these pathways, emotional influences may be reflected in the condition of the skin.

acting systemically or locally, and to nutritional disturbances. But, in addition, many dermatologists are of the opinion that psychogenic factors play a significant role in the production and/or perpetuation of various skin disorders [2] (see Table 2). But just how important a role do the emotions play? There is little disagreement concerning the psychological basis for such conditions as neurotic excoriations or trichotillomania (hair pulling). In other cases, however, the significance of emotional factors would appear to vary widely with the particular disease—and with the particular patient.

Emotional stress may be the most important feature in some reactions, such as pruritus, eczema, urticaria or prurigo. In many patients, tension may cause normal manifestations—such as blushing and sweating—to occur too easily and to be maintained, resulting perhaps in rosacea or hyperhidrosis. In a number of cases, emotional tension apparently acts to set off or aggravate conditions with an obvious viral or bacterial origin, such as herpes recurrens or sycosis barbae; and emotional conflicts increase the risk of skin disorders in a more direct manner, as when compulsive neuroses lead to the excessive use of soap or antiseptic and thus to dermatitis, or when food faddism results in malnutrition and avitaminosis.[3]

The Intractable Itch

Emotional stress probably makes its most damaging contributions to skin disorders when it helps to produce itching, one of the most common, fundamental and important of the symptoms encountered in dermatology. Actually a form of pain, itching can be produced, of course, by almost any noxious stimulus of low intensity.[4] Thus, in certain systemic disorders, severe and persistent itching may result from a disturbance of pain endings by various abnormal substances or metabolites. Similarly, circulating allergens may be responsible for pruritus in many individuals who exhibit no clinical evidence of skin changes. Nevertheless, pruritus, whether localized or generalized, quite often appears to be psychogenic. In anogenital pruritus particularly, psychogenic factors rank first among the various possible causes.[1] Although the mechanism has not yet been clearly established, psychogenic pruritus may generally be ascribed to "some central or peripheral stimulation of an overexcitable neurocutaneous apparatus."[3] Furthermore, in "pruritogenic" individuals, itching frequently appears to arise from unconscious rubbing of the skin. This is seen in *lichen simplex chronicus* (localized neurodermatitis), for instance, in which a scratch-itch-scratch cycle, unconsciously instituted by the patient, may lead to the lichenified "callus" typical of this condition. Psychogenic influences often set the cycle in motion, as indicated by some of the characteristics noted in many patients: pruritus out of proportion to the lesion; individual "itching times" for each patient (while preparing for bed, perhaps, or while relaxing after work); orgiastic scratching followed by relief; and an unconscious tendency to rub the skin.[1]

A prominent psychodynamic feature of this disease, according to some observers, is "suppressed anger, partially discharged through the muscular activity of scratching." [1] (The passive temperament, indicating much repressed emotion, is a familiar type seen in dermatologic practice.[3]) An intense and easily triggered pruritus is also the distinguishing mark of *atopic dermatitis,* and here, too, emotional factors appear to be significant. Rostenberg suggests, however, that psychogenic stimuli are only one of several "inherited determinants. The same inheritance," he observes, "that determines the dry quasi-ichthyotic skin with its vulnerability to pruriginous stimuli" may also favor a "psychogenic maturation that in turn may lead to a commonness of emotional reactions to certain conflictual stimuli." [5]

That many atopic persons do react to conflictual stimuli in a common manner is illustrated by the remarks of patients studied by Schneider.[6]

"Whenever I get mad, my skin itches like fury. I go off by myself or take a walk. I never show my anger."
"I never argue with my mother-in-law or fight with her. I just keep it in. When she was in the hospital for a week, I was calm all that week and didn't scratch."
"When I get mad I keep it to myself but I scratch like the devil. I guess I'd be better off if I exploded but I can't."

Surprisingly similar remarks were offered by patients suffering from *chronic urticaria,* a condition supposedly having an allergic basis, although, as Brodkey [7] points out, in about half of all such cases the causes remain unknown. Some of these patients reported: [8]

"During my high school and college years, each time I had a deadline to meet or a personal problem I couldn't talk about—I'd have an attack of hives."
"Tension at home caused chronic hives for four years, when I was broken out constantly to a greater or lesser degree. Dances and excitement always caused a spell of hives."
"In the summer of 1953, I married my problem and have been without hives, except for two or three times, ever after."

Discussing the typical reactions of such patients, Schneider observes that, while psychological factors are obviously important in the genesis and course of their diseases, there is much disagreement concerning the specific underlying psychic factors. With the particular patients he quotes in his study, he believes that the basic problems were anxiety and guilt connected with hostile aggressive impulses, and he notes with particular interest how "an acute explosive psychic force is so intimately related to an acute explosive reaction in the skin." [6]

Acne Vulgaris—Psychocutaneous?

In many dermatologic conditions, emotional stress is not considered to play an important role. *Acne vulgaris* is one of them. An increase in the size of the sebaceous gland—and a concomitant increase in the amount of sebum secreted—is a normal physiologic change occurring during adolescence. Therefore, some overactivity of the sebaceous glands, excited by hormonal changes, can clearly be expected. Moreover, as Sulzberger and Witten point out, although many acne sufferers themselves blame emotional excitement for a particular outbreak, it is likely that a stressful situation acts only indirectly by causing the patient to neglect health rules. But in some cases, the authors admit, emotional disequilibrium does seem to trigger an exacerbation.[9]

A possible explanation for this phenomenon was advanced by Lorenz, Graham and Wolf after completing experiments designed to correlate sebum production with acne. The investigators noted that, during periods of tranquility, secretion of facial sebum in acne patients was remarkably stable, while during periods of stress, secretion markedly increased (see Fig. 6). Indeed, as compared to non-acne controls, the unique feature of sebaceous gland function in

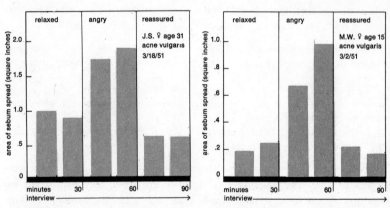

Fig. 6. Results of 90-minute stress experiments on youngest and oldest patients in series. Note increased facial sebum output during "stress" period, in which anger was induced, and decreased output following reassurance.[10]

these patients was lability. Disturbing circumstances produced a prompt fluctuation in facial sebum output.[10] A characteristic emotional pattern was identified in these patients: episodes of anger (with hypersecretion) followed by periods of guilt and depression (with hyposecretion). This suggested to the authors that the following sequence of events was possible: during the *hyposecretory* phase, the relative stasis of sebum might result in changes that could lead to plug formation; during the *hypersecretory* phase, the sudden attempt to secrete sebum in an obstructed duct could lead to impaction of a mass of sebum in the duct; inflammation around this impaction could then cause the papules and pustules typical of acne.

Somatopsychic Aspects—"The Leper Complex"

If many dermatologists doubt that emotional stress contributes to the flare-up of acne, almost all agree that the emotional stress resulting from this disorder cannot be overlooked. Acne, "with its scarring and unsightly lesions on exposed parts of the body, is a disease that can in many cases be sufficiently serious to affect the psyche, even to the point of producing deep-seated and permanent feelings of inferiority and insecurity in the patient."[9] Patients with any unsightly skin disease can be expected to suffer some degree of anxiety and tension. For one thing, such patients have an additional burden to carry. They must cope not only with their own mental and physical distress but also with the real or fancied revulsion of others. The attitude of society toward skin abnormalities does, in fact, tend to be cruel and irrational—possibly, it has been suggested, because of the unconscious feeling that the skin somehow reflects moral purity.[1] Whatever the underlying reason, skin lesions are frequently regarded as "dirty" and "highly contagious," even by the patient himself. Thus, many persons with unsightly lesions in visible areas (such as acne sufferers) may develop a "leper complex" and feel themselves to be loathsome in the extreme.

Diagnosis and Treatment of Psychocutaneous Disorders

Even when a physical basis for the patient's condition cannot be uncovered, the physician cannot always be sure he is dealing with a "skin neurosis." However, certain clues often point to an emotional origin.[1,3,4] For instance, the skin disorder may coincide with an important or disturbing event in the patient's life; the patient may have a past history of psychosomatic conditions or of "nervous breakdowns"; or he may seem highly nervous, sweating or flushing easily or unconsciously rubbing or scratching his skin as he talks. Finally, suspicion may be aroused when there is resistance to, and relapse after, conventional types of therapy.

The patient should be referred for intensive psychiatric treatment when there is evidence of severe neurosis or psychosis, as in delusions of parasitosis. Psychiatric counseling is also recommended in long-standing atopic dermatitis, anal and genital pruritus syndromes, and dermatitis herpetiformis.[1] However, in most cases, referral is not necessary. Most dermatologists and general practitioners find that along with the usual medical regimen, a simple form of supportive psychotherapy—designed to help the patient over rough spots in his life rather than to make him over in any psychological sense—is usually extremely rewarding. And, "by sympathetic counsel, by reassurance and support, the physician reinforces the patient's defenses against anxiety, emphasizes his capacity to get well, encourages self-esteem."[1]

CHAPTER 4 BIBLIOGRAPHY

1. Pillsbury, D. M., Shelley, W. B., and Kligman, A. M.: Dermatology, Philadelphia, Saunders, 1956, pp. 1215 ff.
2. Rostenberg, A., Jr.,: Arch Derm (Chicago) 81:81, 1960.
3. Wittkower, E., and Russell, B.: Emotional Factors in Skin Diseases, New York, Hoeber, 1953.
4. Cormia, F. E.: Skin 1:17, 1962.
5. Rostenberg, A., Jr: Arch Derm (Chicago) 79:692, 1959.
6. Schneider, E.: J Nerv Ment Dis 120:17, 1954.
7. Brodkey, M. H.: Nebraska Med J 46:479, 1961.
8. Mitchell, J. H., Smith, D. L., and Mayers, R. A.: Ann Allerg 15:128, 1957.
9. Sulzberger, M. B., and Witten, V. H.: Med Clin N Amer 43:887, 1959.
10. Lorenz, T. H., Graham, D. T., and Wolf, S.: J Lab Clin Med 41:11, 1953.

ANXIETY AND MAN'S SENSITIVE STOMACH

THE INNARDS of a good many individuals, to paraphrase Kipling, would appear to "brew them perpetual strife." Certainly, the average physician treats daily a variety of gastrointestinal (GI) disorders. And—because the digestive tract, through its autonomic nerve supply, is "especially susceptible to stress-induced alterations in tonicity, motility, secretion, vascularity and excretion" [1]—many of these disorders can be presumed to be influenced, in some degree, by emotional factors.

Some "Gastroemotional" Patterns

That emotions can have a distinct and recognizable effect on digestive activity is hardly a new concept. Our ancestors were not immune to "butterflies" in the stomach. They, too, were well acquainted with some of the unpleasant accompaniments of intense emotion—such as nausea, anorexia, vomiting, diarrhea. More objective evidence of altered gastric function during emotional stress was recorded by Beaumont,[2] as far back as 1833, in his observations on that famous patient, Alexis St. Martin. Among other things, Beaumont ascribed a delay in gastric emptying to the fact that St. Martin was violently angry. Later investigations by Cannon,[4] Todd,[3] Carlson [5] and Pavlov [6] contributed importantly to the growing knowledge of "gastroemotional" patterns.

Todd's extensive radiographic studies, for instance, revealed that sudden or transient emotional upsets were accompanied by decrease in gastric tonus and weak or absent peristalsis. On the other hand, he discovered that an "anxiety complex" was always associated with hyperactivity—a hyperactivity identical to that "which precedes pyloric or duodenal ulcer." [3]

Further evidence of a definite relationship between varied affective states and gastric function was uncovered by Wolf and Wolff [7] in their early studies of a patient with a gastrostomy. Among other patterns that emerged, depression of secretory rates appeared to occur with "reaction of flight or withdrawal from an emotionally charged situation," while accelerations of gastric function followed "internal conflict with an unfulfilled desire for aggression and fighting back." Profound and prolonged emotional disturbances of this kind, accompanied by marked and prolonged increases in gastric motility, secretion and vascularity, often reproduced the picture of gastritis.

In subsequent studies by these investigators and William J. Grace, of four subjects with colonic fistulas, the colon was directly observed to "participate in reactions to stressful like situations." Again, two principal patterns emerged: fear and dejection, associated with *hypofunction* of most of the large intestine—with pallor, relaxation and lack of contractile activity (see Fig. 7); feelings of anger,

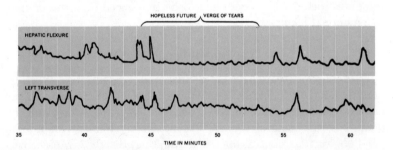

Fig. 7. During interview, subject's feeling of sadness and dejection was associated with prompt cessation of motor activity.[8] Kymographic tracings from balloons in the colon.

resentment, hostility, anxiety and apprehension, associated with *hyperfunction* of the colon—"manifested by increased rhythmic contractile activity and ultimately by intense and frequent waves in the cecum and ascending colon and replacement of rhythmic activity on the left by sustained contraction of longitudinal muscles with shortening and narrowing of the colonic lumen, hypermotility, and hypersecretion of lysozyme" (see Fig. 8).

DIGESTIVE RESPONSE TO STRESS

The authors suggest that these are "protective reaction patterns"

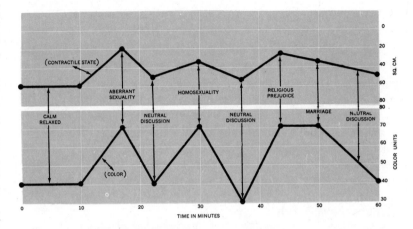

Fig. 8. Variation in subject's colonic function in a short-term experimental setting. During "neutral" conversation associated with calm and cheerfulness, the color and contractile state of the colon were relatively low. Prompt increase in redness and contractile state occurred during anger induced by discussion of topics of conflict.[8] Contractile state is plotted in square cm (length times width) of exposed colonic mucosa.

in which the digestive tract makes the same characteristic physiologic response to psychological threats that it might to other forms of stress. When an individual ingests a poisonous agent, for instance, a physiologic "defense system" is promptly called into play. The stomach's tone and motility diminish, acid secretion decreases, while mucus secretion increases, and the body prepares for vomiting and diarrhea. Similarly, an unacceptable or "disgusting" situation may also be met with gastric hypofunction and readiness to eject a "noxious" agent. "Thus, a person who has 'taken on more than he can handle' or feels inadequate to the demands of his life situation, or a thwarted and passive person filled with hatred, defiance, contempt and the unconscious aim to eject a threatening or overwhelming situation, may have diarrhea." [8]

On the other hand, the pattern of gastric hyperfunction would appear to be related to a subconscious hunger and the desire to be fed and taken care of. Very early, the infant learns to associate fear, anger and anxiety with hunger. In later life, an angry, hungry state may develop in periods of anger and real or imagined deprivation. At these times, the digestive tract prepares itself for an intake of food by increased blood flow motility and acid secretion, and by "a potentially dangerous increase in fragility of the gastric mucosa."

The Variety of GI Complaints

There are a number of other interesting theories to explain the psychogenic basis of certain gastrointestinal disorders. The best known are probably those of Alexander.[9] All have their controversial elements. But, whatever the ultimate reason, many of the varied digestive tract complaints seen by practitioners are quite clearly functional. Most are the result of motor disturbances, with smooth muscle spasms or hyperperistalsis the commonest manifestations. Since these spasms may occur anywhere along the digestive tract, the variety of complaints that they induce is impressive in itself, ranging from globus hystericus at one end of the tract to an "irritable colon" at the other.

Some of the more common clinical syndromes in functional gastrointestinal disorders have been outlined by Wilbur: [10]

MOUTH
    Glossitis; brassy taste
ESOPHAGUS
    Hysterical dysphagia
    Globus
    Plummer-Vinson syndrome
    Cardiospasm
STOMACH AND DUODENUM
    Functional dyspepsia
    Aerophagia
    Functional vomiting
    Anorexia nervosa
    Nausea
    Pseudo-ulcer
    Pyrosis

BILIARY TRACT
    Postcholecystectomy syndrome
    Biliary dyskinesia
SMALL BOWEL
    Hypermotility
    Hypomotility
    (Deficiency disease pattern)
COLON
    Irritable colon
    (Splenic flexure syndrome)
    Diarrhea
    Constipation
    Functional or hysterical bloating
GI TRACT AS A WHOLE

The varied changes in gastric function which accompany emotional stages (changes which, according to Ivy, Grossman and Bachrach, should be termed *emotogenic* [11]) may lead to disturbances that are initially functional but potentially structural. This is particularly true of emotogenic alterations of vasomotor, vascular and secretory functions of the GI tract. These latter may result in hyperemia and hypersecretion or ischemia and hyposecretion of the mucosa. Because such conditions evoke erosion or actual ulceration of mucosa,[12] they may precipitate—certainly aggravate—such disorders as gastritis, hyperacidity, peptic ulcer and ulcerative colitis.

In peptic ulcer, for instance, stress-induced alterations, particularly in the secretion of acid gastric juice, have long been con-

sidered important contributory factors. A principal reason for this
assumption is the demonstration by a number of observers that
emotional stress acts as a stimulus for the increased production of

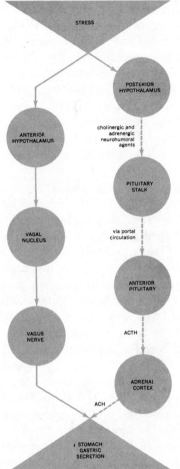

Fig. 9. Schema for the action
of stress on gastric secretion.[14]

gastric acid and pepsin.[7, 8, 13, 14, 15] Shay and his co-workers [14] have,
in fact, worked out a schema for the possible pathway by which
emotional stress influences gastric secretion (see Fig. 9). Emotional
stress, they suggest, acting on the posterior hypothalamic nuclei,
causes the transmission of cholinergic and adrenergic neurohumoral
agents to the pituitary stalk. From here, the agents reach the ante-
rior pituitary by way of the portal circulation and cause the release
of ACTH, which, in turn, is followed by release of adrenal corticoids
to stimulate gastric secretory cells.

In addition to stress-induced gastric hypersecretion, other factors associated with stress reactions, such as tissue changes, probably encourage weakening of local tissue resistance. Thus, as Ivy and his associates point out, anxiety or psychic trauma can be considered an "excitatory cause of peptic ulcer in persons predisposed to ulcer." Moreover, psychic factors play a role not only in the initiation of an ulcer, but in its recurrence, as demonstrated by the increased incidence of perforations and hemorrhages seen when a population is exposed to an environment "in which sustained anxiety is an outstanding component." Nevertheless, the authors observe that "since peptic ulcer can still occur after vagus or splanchnic nerves are cut, it would appear that emotional factors that use these pathways can operate only as an excitatory and not as a basic cause of peptic ulcer." [11]

That other elements besides stress must be present before actual ulceration takes place is borne out by the investigations of Grace, Wolf and Wolff.[8] Of particular importance, they suggest, is the personality of the individual. Two of their patients, for instance—who tended to suppress their feelings of anger and hostility and seemed unable to act or verbalize their emotions during stress—had an engorged, hyperemic, fragile colon more often and for far greater lengths of time than two others. These were the patients who had ulcerative colitis. A third patient, who was able to express his feelings readily, displayed comparatively less frequent and less sustained colonic hyperfunction. His bowel was free of disease. The fourth patient, who tended to react to major problems by becoming low in spirits and depressed, was also free from disease. Characteristically, this man displayed colonic hypofunction and constipation.

The investigators concluded that sustained episodes of hyperfunction in predisposed individuals probably accounted for the damage seen in ulcerative colitis. In their experience, protracted hyperfunction seemed to render the colonic mucosa more susceptible to injury and was, in fact, even associated with the spontaneous appearance of petechial hemorrhages in the mucosa. In addition, the rise in lysozyme concentration that also was found to accompany emotional tension "may contribute to the damage of mucous membrane and expose its surface to the action of irritating fecal contents or invasion of indigenous bacterial flora.[8]

Essentials of Treatment

With our current diagnostic methods, including radiologic, gastroscopic and cytologic studies, such organic conditions as peptic ulcer, cancer and biliary tract disease can be more readily identified, and, in the absence of organic disease, the presence of functional disorders can often "be determined at an early stage and adequate treatment of the psychic and somatic phases be inaugurated." [16]

Successful management of functional GI disorders, according to McHardy and his associates,[1] encompasses dietetic therapy, office counseling, and the application of measures directed toward correction of neuromuscular and secretory functions. "An attitude of sincere interest and understanding on the part of the physician, instead of impatience with these psychogenic disturbances, can be extremely helpful," the authors suggest, and add that newer psychopharmacologic agents, "when used judiciously, improve the patient's outlook and are of great assistance in creating 'insight' and effecting 'cure'."

Many of these measures apply equally to the management of organic disease. "The majority of patients with either organic or functional gastrointestinal disease," points out Charles W. Hock, "require psychosomatic therapy regardless of whether the mental component is the primary or secondary symptom." [17]

CHAPTER 5 BIBLIOGRAPHY

1. McHardy, G., et al.: Postgrad Med 31:346, 1962.
2. Beaumont, W.: Experiments and Observations on the Gastric Juice and the Physiology of Digestion, Plattsburg (NY), F. P. Allen, 1833.
3. Todd, T. W.: Behavior Patterns of the Alimentary Tract, Baltimore, Williams & Wilkins, 1930.
4. Cannon, W. B.: Amer J Med Sci 137:480, 1909.
5. Carlson, A. J.: Amer J Physiol 31:151, 1912.
6. Pavlov, I.: The Work of the Digestive Glands, London, C. Griffin & Co., 1910.
7. Wolf, S., and Wolff, H. G.: Human Gastric Function, New York, Oxford, 1947.
8. Grace, W. J., Wolf, S., and Wolff, H. G.: The Human Colon, New York, Hoeber, 1951.
9. Alexander, F.: Psychoanal Quart 3:501, 1934.
10. Wilbur, D. L.: Med Clin N Amer 40:329, 1956.
11. Ivy, A. C., Grossman, M. I., and Bachrach, W. H.: Peptic Ulcer, Philadelphia, Blakiston, 1950.
12. Smith, V. H.: Psychosom Med 4:85, 1963.
13. Mittlemann, B., and Wolff, H. G.: Psychosom Med 4:5, 1942.
14. Shay, H., et al.: J Appl Physiol 12:461, 1958.
15. Seymour, C. T., and Weinberg, J. A.: JAMA 171:1193, 1959.
16. Jordan, S. M.: Med Clin N Amer 40:271, 1956.
17. Hock, C. W.: J New Drugs 1:90, 1961.

ANXIETY AND PAIN

A PASSION of the soul—this is how Aristotle, some 2,400 years ago, classified pain, specifically excluding the sensation of pain from his doctrine of the five senses: vision, hearing, taste, smell and touch.[1] His interpretation anticipates today's recognition of the emotional component in the reaction to pain. However, it was not until the nineteenth century that the modern approach to pain evolved. This approach:

a. acknowledges the specificity of pain as a sensation—different from pressure, cold or warmth,[1, 2]

b. sees the perception of pain and the reaction to pain as two distinct and fundamental aspects of the pain experience—assigning to the latter, the psychic experience, as important a role as to the former, the sensory perception.[1, 3-6]

Pain Perception vs Reaction

The discrepancy between the perception of pain and the reaction to it has been traced and demonstrated in assiduous experimental work on the nature of pain by Harold Wolff and his associates at Cornell.[1, 8, 9] Apparently, the ability to perceive pain depends on the intactness of relatively simple and primitive nerve connections, while the reaction to pain is a complex physiopsychologic process that involves the highest cognitive functions of the individual.[1, 7] Actually, what is experienced and reported by the patient is a psychological phenomenon—a blend of what the patient feels, thinks and does about the pain he perceives.[7] These strong feeling states of anguish and displeasure may predominate in the experience of pain to the point where they become, to the sufferer, the most relevant aspect of his pain.[1] The *response* to pain *per se* then assumes major proportions and, at times, may become a greater threat to survival than the original assault.[3]

A Highly Personal Affair

The individual differences in reaction to pain depend on not only the emotional state of the patients but also their past life experiences and associations, conscious and unconscious, with the situations in which the painful stimulus arises.[3, 10-11] Since the experience of pain and the sensory experiences from which it evolves are part of the biologic equipment whereby the individual learns about his environment and his body, and since it performs a special function as an indicator of damage to body parts, pain plays an important role in the total psychological development of the individual. In the child's emotional growth, pain and relief of pain enter into the formation of interpersonal relations and into the concepts of good and bad, reward and punishment, success and failure. Indeed, pain joins other affects in occupying a key position in the regulation of the total psychic economy.[4]

Aring cites the case of the patient with trigeminal neuralgia. Although exquisitely localized, there is no question that even in this condition, as in many others, "the sensation of pain may spread to become what we may term an 'emotion.'"[12]

> Pain has an element of blank;
> It cannot recollect
> When it began, or if there were
> A day when it was not.
>
> It has no future but itself,
> Its infinite realms contain
> Its past, enlightened to perceive
> New periods of pain.
>
> *Emily Dickinson*

Anxiety and Pain: Vicious Cycle

Prominent among the emotions that influence the intensity of the pain reaction is anxiety. Pain is almost always linked with and potentiated by anxiety. For one thing, a high level of anxiety can lower the pain threshold and increase the subjective reaction to pain [13, 14]: the anxious individual has less tolerance for pain and its effects are apt to be more devastating to him. Pain, in turn, can also produce or increase anxiety.

Such anxiety frequently focuses on the sufferer's capacity to tolerate pain or on its special significance to him. "How long is this pain going to last? Will I be able to tolerate it? Does it mean serious illness—or even worse?" Such anxious questions, heard often, betray the patient's emotional turmoil and reveal the reciprocal influence pain and anxiety tend to have on each other.[14] A vicious cycle is initiated, which includes pain as a source of anxiety, anxiety as a factor in increased pain, and increased pain as an inciter of further anxiety.[11]

Beecher,[15] who compared the pain of war wounds with the pain of comparable surgical interventions in civilian life, noted the relevance of the psychological situation to the severity of the pain reaction: in a situation where the wound connoted disaster (civil surgery), lesser wounds were associated with more pain and required more narcotics than on the battlefield, where the wound meant replacement of desperate anxiety (death on the battlefield) by a far lesser worry—the wound.

In an experimental observation demonstrating the relationship of the psychological climate to the intensity of the pain reaction, Schottstaedt cites the different results obtained in the same patient with the cold pressor test, depending on the situation: "The patient who is anxious, knowing that this test may determine whether he is to be operated upon or not, may have a very marked change in blood pressure and find the experience intensely painful. On another day, when this decision no longer hangs in the balance, the same test in the same patient may elicit little elevation of blood pressure and no pain." [11]

Pains Without Cause?

Anxiety, aroused by the anticipation of pain, may evoke a response before any pain is actually felt. Witness the child who cries at an uplifted hand or the adult who winces at the sight of the dentist's drill. People who are apprehensive about dental work are more apt to experience severe pain than those who are not.[11] Anxious anticipation of pain that "may itself be more painful than the actual pain of the prospective procedure" [14] can also be observed, for example, in the patient scheduled for a minor surgical procedure.

Another anxiety-creating aspect of pain is its symbolic significance: laymen have learned to think of pain as a warning; occasionally they may even think of it as a punishment. If the pain is of a common variety—a headache or an arthralgia—the patient may not fear its consequences. But if the pain is strange to him, its anxiety-creating potential can be great.[16] Even normal visceral sensations, which otherwise would pass unnoticed, may become painful when there is neurotic overconcern with health; and the threshold of sensation is heightened to the point of painful perception.[14] "If I only knew what it was and that it would not turn into anything, I'd forget it," such an anxious patient may say in his plea for your reassurance.[17]

Any Body System Vulnerable

While psychogenic magnification of a physiogenic pain may occur in any body organ,[6] this process is perhaps most strikingly exemplified in the *anginal* patient. The threatening knowledge that his heart is involved triggers in the anginal sufferer new anxieties that may lead to still more frequent attacks. Here, emotional stress, unlike physical exertion, seems to exert only harmful action. While pointing to the need for more direct observations, T. R. Harrison mentions this possible explanation of the mechanism involved: emotional stress, he says, "Presumably . . . either causes constriction of collaterals or, at least, fails to open them in proportion to the increase in myocardial oxygen need." [18]

Another body area whose functions are related intimately to emotional life is the upper *gastrointestinal* tract.[19] The role of emotional features in the patient with peptic ulcer finds confirmation in objective pain-measuring studies of such patients: the observers considered both pain perception and pain reaction threshold of peptic ulcer sufferers to be similar to those of psychoneurotic patients,[20] emphasizing the importance of emotional disturbance in not only the pathogenesis but also the course and management of peptic ulcer.

Childbirth "is another instance in which the effect of anxiety is commonly recognized" [11] as a factor in pain. And, while not the primary cause of the pain, anguish certainly plays a major role in a woman's approach to excessive *dysmenorrheic* discomforts [21] or to excessive *menopausal* disturbances.[22] In the *arthritic* patient, fluctuations in the intensity of pain following periods of severe emotional stress are a matter of common observation.[23]

Leap from Emotional to Physical

Emotional factors may provoke painful conditions by a mechanism that is entirely central.[5, 24] Such is the case in the so-called "true psychogenic pain" and in hysterical conversion pain—situations in which the pain is likely to have purely symbolic significance to the patient. This mechanism contrasts with that of psychosomatic pain, where the pain is mediated through peripheral mechanisms and is the direct result of an organic or functional alteration.[5, 24]

Also, in purely psychogenic pain, only the psychotherapeutic approach holds promise, while in psychosomatic conditions, medicinal therapy directed at the affected organ may bring immediate relief of acute pain. "Purely psychogenic pain may take any form and may be of any degree of quality." [16] Common examples are "psychogenic" headaches [24] or backaches.[25] When manifested as "cardiac neurosis," psychogenic pain poses the extremely delicate problem of differential diagnosis from true anginal pain.[26]

Pain as a symptom of conversion hysteria must fulfill the usual prerequisites of this disease. As with other conversion reactions, hysterical pain is considered to result from psychic conflicts that, instead of giving rise to anxiety, secure symbolic external expression [14] —by a leap, as it were, from the emotional to the physical.[10] Typically, hysterical pain is communicated in a patient's expression, posture or behavior, no matter what he's doing. This is not so with psychosomatic pains, which may be suffered without ostentation.[5] Another point of difference: conversion reactions are effected largely over areas innervated by the voluntary nervous system, whereas psychosomatic pain, for the most part, is caused by autonomic action.[13]

Borderlands of Neurophysiology and Psychiatry

The phenomena of "phantom limb" and phantom pain, though common, continue as "always surprising findings in medical and surgical practice." [24] They demonstrate clearly the emotional roots of pain reactions and the importance of central areas in pain formation. A common interpretation holds the phantom limb to be a consequence of the proprioceptive body-image that every individual develops in childhood,[27, 28] It is the reluctance to give up a cherished part of the self; and the pain is the discharge of feeling over the loss.[24]

Another observation from the borderlands of neurophysiology and psychiatry is the power of hypnosis to lower or eliminate overt and subjective response to painful stimuli. Hypnosis has been used, though to a limited extent, in minor surgical procedures, diagnostic exploration, dental operations, and obstetrics. Hypnoanalgesia is assumed to act by focusing the patient's interest away from himself.[29] Perhaps this is akin to what happens when attention is diverted during pain in the waking state—a recurring theme in reports on pain relief wrought in strange lands and cultures (see Fig. 10).

Fig. 10. Preoccupation can lessen the awareness of pain. "One must realize," says Chen in a discussion of analgesic methods, "that anxiety, mood and obsession frequently cause the sufferer to exaggerate his pain, but distraction, preoccupation and concentration make him forget his pain."

In emphasizing his point, he tells this story: "Centuries ago, a general, Kuan Kung, was wounded in the arm after a furious battle. It became infected. He went to see the famous surgeon, Hua Tu. . . . The abscess had to be lanced. Knowing the general was a good checker player, the surgeon called in a champion to engage him in a game. In the middle of their mental contest the surgeon sucessfully opened the abscess and drained a large quantity of pus. . . . No pain was felt. And the general was ready for another battle." [30]

Pain and the Reticular Activating System

Wondrous as they may appear, such reports seem to have their physiologic counterpart in observations on the screening activity of the effector neurons in the reticular activating system. This activity exercises a considerable and selective control over the signals transmitted by the afferent and efferent nerves. In a series of ingenious cat experiments, Hernandez-Peon and his colleagues [31] have shown that electrically recorded brain wave spikes, generated by a minor stimulus, dramatically decreased when the animal was presented with a major stimulus. This demonstrates, says Wooldridge, that "nerve signals produced by extraneous stimuli do not merely *seem* to be lessened when we concentrate; they *are* lessened." [32] Apparently, in the conscious as well as in the unconscious response-selection process, "volume-control" signals are generated in the reticular system to reduce sensitivity to uninteresting or irrelevant stimuli and thereby achieve "mental concentration." The principle has found tentative application in the dentist's office, where the patient's anxious attention to painful manipulations is diverted: when listening to recordings of sounds of waves breaking on the shore, patients reported markedly less pain and discomfort. It has been suggested that this kind of sound, because it covers a wide range of the audible frequency spectrum, may involve a correspondingly large number of neurons in the reticular activating system; this involvement may be responsible for the unusual effectiveness of such a sound in turning down the "volume control" in the nerve circuits that conduct pain to the higher centers of the brain.[32]

The simple observation that the intensity of two pains existing separately at the same time is no greater than that of the more intense of the two—

$$1 \text{ severe pain} + 1 \text{ light pain} = 1 \text{ severe pain}—$$

is another demonstration of the emotional self-regulation of pain reactions. Apparently, the existence of one pain raises the threshold for perception of another.[33] This effect was noted by Hippocrates, who may have observed a fellow Greek bite his lips in pain or drive his fingernails into his palms.

Lessening Emotional Overreaction to Pain

"In approaching the treatment of pain," states Bonica, "it is desirable to differentiate among that which is primarily structural, primarily psychologic and primarily physiologic."[7] In somatic pain with considerable psychologic overlay, the emotional overreaction may demand therapeutic attention, in addition to pain-relieving measures *per se*, because an "analgesic may be more effective in a cooperative, than a doubtful, patient."[30] Tranquilizing therapy, as an adjunct to analgesics, has been found effective in lessening the emotional response to pain: with apprehension and anxiety relieved, the patient's mental outlook improves and he may assume a more rational attitude toward both his pain and its cause.

However, when the psychic factor is significant, as in many psychophysiologic disorders, or when the pain is related to personality factors without demonstrable physiologic changes, then the treatment of the psychologic problem becomes paramount[7]: any of the forms of emotional support—plain reassurance of psychotherapy, calming drugs, social measures—will make the pain more bearable and may at the same time deal with the underlying emotional factors. As Hardy, Wolff and Goodell, who pioneered in the distinction between pain perception and pain reaction, remind us: "Those who would deal with pain as therapists must concern themselves with reactions to pain."[3]

CHAPTER 6 BIBLIOGRAPHY

1. Wolff, H. G., and Wolf, S.: Pain, ed 2, Springfield (Ill), Thomas, 1958, pp. 11 ff.
2. Boring, E. G.: *in* Hardy, J. D., Wolff, H. G., and Goodell, H., eds.: Pain Sensations and Reactions, Baltimore, Williams & Wilkins, 1952, pp. v ff.
3. Hardy, J. D., Wolff, H. G., and Goodell, H., eds.: *Ibid.*, pp. 24, 386 ff.
4. Engel, G. L.: Occup Med 3:249, 1961.
5. Meares, A.: The Management of the Anxious Patient, Philadelphia, Saunders, 1963, pp. 405 ff.
6. Walters, A.: Appl Ther 5:853, 1963.
7. Bonica, J. J.: GP 33:107. 1966.
8. Schumacher, G. A., *et al.*: Science 92:110, 1940.
9. Wolff, H. G., Hardy, J. D., and Goodell, H.: J Pharmacol Exp Ther 75:38, 1942.
10. Rangell, L.: Psychosom Med 15:22, 1953.
11. Schottstaedt, W. W.: Psychophysiologic Approach in Medical Practice, Chicago, Yr Bk Pub, 1960, pp. 89 ff.
12. Aring, C. D.: Med Clin N Amer, November, 1958, p. 1467.
13. Bash, N. P.: Delaware Med J 37:116, 1965.
14. Laughlin, H. P.: The Neuroses in Clinical Practice, Philadelphia, Saunders, 1956, pp. 62 ff, 244, 522.
15. Beecher, H. K.: JAMA 161:1609, 1956.
16. Modell, W.: Relief of Symptoms, ed 2, St. Louis, Mosby, 1961, pp. 77 ff.
17. Alvarez, W. C.: The Neuroses, Philadelphia, Saunders, 1955, p. 87.
18. Harrison, T. R.: Arch Intern Med (Chicago) 117:323, 1966.
19. Kolb, L. C.: Mayo Clin Proc 28:402, 1953.
20. Schilling, R. E., and Musser, M. J.: Amer J Med Sci 218:207, 1949.
21. Sturgis, S. H., and Menzer-Benaron, D.: *in* Sturgis, S. H., ed.: The Gynecologic Patient, New York, Grune, 1962, pp. 66 ff.
22. Schilling, R. F., and Musser, M. J.: Amer J Med Sci 218:204, 1949.
23. Coggeshall, H. C.: Med Clin N Amer, November, 1958, p. 1603.
24. Hoffling, C. K.: Textbook of Psychiatry for Medical Practice, Philadelphia, Lippincott, 1963, pp. 153, 161 ff.
25. Gottschalk, L. A.: GP 33:91, 1966.
26. Harris, A. W.: Med Clin N Amer, November, 1958, p. 1511.
27. Weiss, E., and English, O. S.: Psychosomatic Medicine, ed 3, Philadelphia, Saunders, 1957, p. 529.
28. Noyes, A. P., and Kolb, L. C.: Modern Clinical Psychiatry, ed 6, Philadelphia, Saunders, 1963, p. 409.
29. Wolfberg, L. R.: *in* Arieti, S., ed.: American Handbook of Psychiatry, vol 2, New York, Basic, 1959, pp. 1470 ff.
30. Chen, K. K.: Med Clin N Amer, March, 1950, p. 369.
31. Hernandez-Peon, R., Scherrer, H., and Jouvet, M.: Science 123:331, 1956.
32. Wooldridge, D. E.: The Machinery of the Brain, New York, McGraw-Hill, 1963, pp. 140 ff.
33. Genuine Works of Hippocrates: Translated by Francis Adams, London, 1859.

ANXIETY AND ALLERGY

~~~~~~

SIXTY YEARS ago allergy was first defined immunologically as altered or hyper-reactivity. It is now time to broaden this definition to include what we now know of *emotional* hyperreactivity. . . . "[1] In making this appeal for the inclusion of emotional factors in the pathogenesis of allergy, Doctors Rapaport and McGovern also delineate the significance of such an approach. It is urged, they state, "not in order to decrease our study of immunology, but in order to expand our knowledge to allergic disease in areas that have hitherto defied explanation."

How do emotional factors operate to influence allergy? Can asthma, eczema, hay fever or hives appear from purely emotional causes? The interpretations of the relationship between psyche and soma in allergy are numerous. Among the interpreters, a small minority holds that the allergic response is produced by emotional stress as the primary factor. Wolff, in particular, has given examples of experimentally induced nasal congestive symptoms and "asthmatic" attacks produced in individuals by submitting them to periods of anxiety and stress.[2]

Conceivably, says Meares, in certain cases of allergy "the allergic response may operate merely as a factor in determining the site of the psychosomatic reaction. . . ."[3] The majority of medical observers feel, however, that the truth lies in neither a strictly psychologic nor a rigidly somatic approach. They agree that while allergy is initiated by an antigen-antibody reaction, anxiety and emotional stress also play a role, and that this role is one of a. activating, b. aggravating, or c. complicating this existing allergic mechanism and its clinical symptomatology.[1, 4-6]

Anxiety Activates Allergic Reactivity

That anxiety, fear, grief and other emotional states alter the excitability of the autonomic nervous system and have profound effects on the physiology of the lungs, blood vessels, heart rate, adrenalin secretion and similar functions, is a well-established fact. Severe anxiety states, for instance, are known often to cause dis-

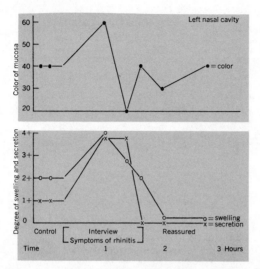

Fig. 11. Test of 21-year-old female with 12-year history of hay fever and strongly positive skin and eye test for ragweed sensitivity. For the investigation, she forwent her yearly immunization therapy.

Symptoms developed during the pollen season, but on the day of the experiment the patient was symptom-free at a pollen count of 14 gr/cu yd air. During the interview, as she expressed misgivings about participating in the experiment and about the way that it was being conducted, she became tense, anxious, restless, and developed typical symptoms of hay fever coryza in nose and eyes. The initial color increase (to 60) later gave way to rebound pallor (20). All symptoms subsided at the end of the interview, as she regained her confidence and composure, based on the experimenter's reassurances. (Adapted from Holmes, T. H., Treuting, T., and Wolff, H. G.[9])

turbances of the respiratory, gastrointestinal, and sleep mechanisms.[4] In view of these facts, "it is not at all surprising," writes Feinberg, that the effects of emotion "may play a part in the production of the allergic attack."[7] In the words of Walter C. Alvarez, so finely can nervousness and fatigue set the allergic trigger "that it can almost go off by itself."[8] Experimental studies in patients suffering from allergic disease have demonstrated the activation of symptomatology during periods of induced anxiety and emotional stress. The results of such experiments in hay fever and asthma are given in Figures 11 and 12.

Anxiety Aggravates Allergic Symptomatology

Acute emotional stress and chronic or anxiety states not only precipitate but also exacerbate clinical symptomatology in the allergic

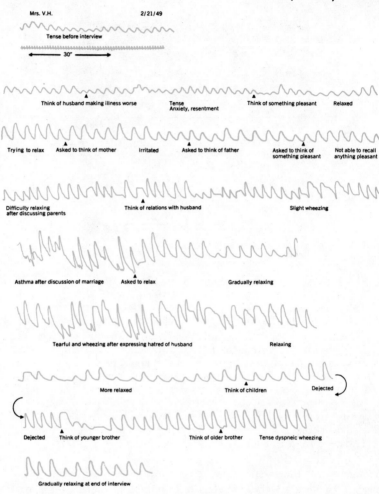

Fig. 12. Pneumographic test on housewife, 35, with chronic bronchial asthma for 15 years, difficult emotional relationship to mother and to elder brother, married unhappily and worried about her children. Patient herself is aware of a close relationship between emotional disturbances and attacks of asthma: "the least thought," she says, "will bring asthma." Recordings during stressful interview show periods of resentment associated with changes in respiratory movements, dyspnea, wheezing and the expectoration of bronchial mucus not expectorated at other times. (Adapted from Stevenson, I.[10])

patient.[1, 11-13] Their influence may extend to the character, frequency and severity of the allergic paroxysms. Criep points to the common observation of severe asthmatic attacks developing in the patient when under heavy emotional strain, and of flare-ups of dermatoses, under similar circumstances, in the patient suffering from atopic dermatitis.[14]

"Under the impact of anxiety, fear, or some other emotional explosion," he explains, "the cough, dyspnea, or pruritus becomes unbearable. The patient's irritability increases, he becomes sleepless, loses his appetite and weight, and becomes very ill." [14] And it is only with improvement in his psychogenic disturbance that allergic treatment again becomes effective.

Anxiety Complicates Allergy Management

Although allergy may be greatly influenced by psychosomatic factors, the reverse is also true. Indeed, the somatopsychic reaction [15] —the influence of the allergic disorder on the emotional make-up of the patient—may have grievous influences on the course of the disease. Feinberg considers the profound effect the allergy may have on the nervous system the "most important relationship" between the two.[7]

Citing the problems of repeated asthma attacks, the wakefulness at night, the intense itching, and the discomforts of many other allergic conditions, he writes that these effects of the allergic disease "can and do produce anxieties, frustrations and nervousness." [16] The child, for instance, who has been up nights with asthma, has been pampered by the family and has found a means of escape from onerous duties, is almost bound to develop an abnormal personality, be quarrelsome, develop anxiety complexes or, in an attempt to overcome inferiority feelings, grow up into a "bully." [7]

Finally, there are the cases in which emotional conflicts can prolong the clinical course of an existing allergic condition.[15] Sanger has made a successful search for psychic "onset situations" in a number of patients, where allergic syndromes (that were in a state of remission) recurred with an intensification of symptoms, when severe anxiety states supervened [4]; job loss, draft board notification, and arrested menses were among the eliciting events. Apprehensive emotions have even been observed to trigger attacks in an established allergy by what might be a conditioned reflex mechanism (examples: the opera-goer responding with his typical hay fever symptoms on viewing a blooming meadow in "Faust," the patient suffering an attack of sneezing at the sight of paper roses).[17]

Asthma, "Suppressed Cry"

Of all allergic conditions, asthma is perhaps that in which, in certain patients, the psychic influence appears most predominant and etiologically significant.[18] Even Hippocrates noted that the asthmatic must guard against anger. In 1922, Weiss postulated that asthmatic episodes in the child are precipitated by separation from the mother. This concept has been elaborated by French and Alexander.[19-21] In a psychoanalytic study of adults and children with allergic predisposition, they emphasized certain specific psychodynamic factors relevant to the onset of asthmatic attacks; they observed that the asthmatic child, unable to resolve dependency upon his mother, experienced anxiety whenever threatened with separation from her.

While this separation anxiety of the child may involve actual physical separation, more frequently it is the danger of estrangement from the parental figure, due to some beckoning temptation. In such a situation, these observers feel, the asthma attacks seem to have the significance of a suppressed cry. In this context it may be worth remembering that in some asthmatics it is most difficult to ascertain the allergen [17]—patients, for example, in whom allergenic agents cause symptoms but fail to give a positive skin reaction, or allergens, while giving a skin reaction, do not precipitate symptoms.[22] It is also an observed therapeutic fact that changes in emotional environment sometimes control asthma—as in a child "whose 'intractable' asthma is miraculously cured by parentectomy." [1] Likewise, the effectiveness of a change of climate in relieving asthma has been interpreted in some cases as due, in reality, to removal from a domestic problem situation rather than an unsuitable climate.[22]

The Frightened Asthmatic

Whether asthma in its original phase has been precipitated by allergic or by psychologic factors (or a combination of the two), in fully developed asthma anxiety remains as a most important psychosomatic element throughout the course of the disease. Because of their inability to breathe, many asthmatic patients have the feeling of suffocation and impending death. "It is only natural that they manifest symptoms of anxiety and restlessness between attacks, because they are apprehensive . . . when the next attack will come and whether they will survive." [5] Furthermore, "fear of a mild attack may precipitate one of major intensity and sometimes even one of status asthmaticus." [22] Thus, psychotropic drugs have been found useful by many physicians in the long-range management of their asthmatic patients.

Skin Allergies: Six Clues to Anxiety

The skin being "the most expressive organ for demonstation of psychological disturbances," [23] it is not difficult to see why the psychic element is also often clearly in evidence in allergic dermatosis and its various forms—eczema, dermatitis, urticaria.[1, 12, 16, 17, 23] Characteristic of some of these cases is their running a course of waxing and waning intensity according to various stresses to which the patient is subject.[3] The "fact that the skin condition deteriorates with additional stress, which also is manifested in other signs of anxiety, is clear evidence of the importance of the emotional factor" and of the need for treating the psychological element lest the condition continue to run this fluctuating course.[3] Urging physicians to be alert to emotional situations that may have produced exacerbations in skin allergies, Sanger offers the following six clues [23]:

1. The location of the lesion may be atypical—e.g., a dermatitis confined to only one finger.
2. The character of the lesion may be bizarre—not conforming to the physiological pattern of the nerve and blood supply of the ailing part, the "glove and stocking" effect.
3. The onset of a dermatitis may be connected with an emotionally charged event—skin lesions following loss of employment, e.g., or the death of a parent.
4. Self-limiting lesions may persist or recur—urticaria occurring only in the evening, when the patient returns from work, or only on weekends, when the patient stays at home.
5. Laughter or tears while telling a history may be inappropriate.
6. Symptoms may start concurrently with the onset of a state of anxiety or depression.

Emotional Desensitization

Prigal, in a 1960 study sponsored by the New York Allergy Society, considers the psyche as the third factor involved in the highly complex interplay of forces instrumental in the allergic syndrome—the allergen and the infection being the other two (Fig. 13). "Clinically," he states, "the allergist who relies exclusively on the skin test, without considering the part that infection or the psyche may play in allergic disease, is apt to be severely frustrated in his practice." [15]

A program for such a "total" treatment of the allergic patient, Sanger feels,[23] should consider:

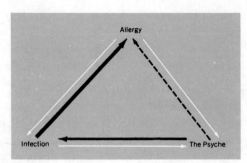

Fig. 13. Diagrammatic interpretation of the interplay of forces thought to be involved in the allergic syndrome—each force able not only to produce disease, but, possibly, to initiate vicious cycles or chain-type reactions. The heavier arrows indicate a more positive force; the broken arrow, a force suspected but not proved. (Adapted from Prigal, S. J.[15])

1. *Antiallergic needs* (allergic work-up, dietary restrictions, environmental controls, hypoimmunization),

2. *Pharmacologic needs* (oral medications such as antihistamines, antispasmodics, sympathomimetics, steriods; local applications, vaporizers, antibiotics), and also

3. *Psychologic needs* (ventilation, reassurance, environment manipulation, counseling, supportive therapy), and

4. *Psychopharmacologic drugs* (tranquilizers, antidepressants).

In about one third of allergic cases, Dr. Sanger states, psychological investigation can be rewarding.

CHAPTER 7 BIBLIOGRAPHY

1. Rapaport, H. G., and McGovern, J. P.: Editorial, Ann Allergy 23:447, 1965.
2. Wolff, H. G.: Stress and Disease, Springfield (Ill), Thomas, 1953, pp. 97 ff.
3. Meares, A.: The Management of the Anxious Patient, Philadelphia, Saunders, 1963, pp. 440, 470 ff.
4. Sanger, M. D.: Ann Allergy 22:418, 1964.
5. Taub, S. J.: Psychosomatics 2:349, 1961.
6. Rapaport, H. G.: Ann Allergy 22:541, 1964.
7. Feinberg, S. M.: Allergy in Practice, Chicago, Yr Bk Pub, 1949, pp. 90 ff.
8. Alvarez, W. C.: The Neuroses, Philadelphia, Saunders, 1955, pp. 466 ff.
9. Holmes, T. H., Treuting, T., and Wolff, H. G.: A Res Nerv & Ment Dis 29:545, 1950.
10. Stevenson, I. A.: A Res Nerv & Ment Dis 29:596, 1950.
11. Sanger, M. D.: Ann Allergy 20:705, 1962.
12. Tuft, L.: Clinical Allergy, ed 2, Philadelphia, Lea, 1949, pp. 126 ff., 518.
13. McGovern, J. P., et al.: Ann Allergy 18:1193, 1960.

14. Criep, L. H.: Essentials of Allergy, Philadelphia, Lippincott, 1945, pp. 107 ff.
15. Prigal, S. J., ed.: Fundamentals of Modern Allergy, New York, Blakiston, McGraw-Hill, 1960, pp. 2, 82 ff.
16. Feinberg, S. M.: Living with Your Allergy, Philadelphia, Lippincott, 1958, pp. 42, 127 ff.
17. Urbach, E., and Gottlieb, P. M.: Allergy, ed 2, New York, Grune, 1946, pp. 52, 74 ff., 570 ff., 750 ff.
18. Sugihara, H., Ishihara, K., and Noguchi, H.: Ann Allergy 23:422, 1965.
19. French, T. M., and Alexander, F.: Psychogenic Factors in Bronchial Asthma, parts 1 and 2, Psychosomatic Medicine Monograph IV, Washington (DC), Nat Res Council, 1941.
20. Selesnick, S.: Med Times 93:269, 1965.
21. Weiss, E., and English, O. S.: Psychosomatic Medicine, ed 3, Philadelphia, Saunders, 1957, p. 433.
22. Hansel, F. K.: Clinical Allergy, St. Louis, Mosby, 1953, pp. 605 ff., 702.
23. Sanger, M. D.: Ann Allergy 21:530, 1963.

ANXIETY AND OBESITY

T HERE IS a widespread feeling among physicians that treating obesity would be quite simple if overweight patients were more cooperative. In most cases, it is reasoned, all the patient has to do in order to achieve predictable weight loss is to stick to his diet; soon he would look and feel substantially better. Nevertheless, despite sound medical advice and the pleas of family and friends, the obese patient quite often remains singularly uncooperative. As a discouraged colleague once observed to Bruch, "All they lose is the sheet with the carefully calculated diet." [1]

"Simple Obesity" and Its Complex Foundation

Investigators, therefore, have been forced to conclude that "simple obesity," as opposed to conditions of obesity with a demonstrable organic basis, is a good deal more complicated than it appears. As Bruch points out, early workers in this field appear to have overlooked the fact that although obesity may be caused "simply" by overeating and underactivity, "the drives for food and activity are regulated by mechanisms which are not at all simple." [1]

Among the many structures concerned with the mechanism of regulating food intake (see Fig. 14), the most important is a system of central areas, some cortical and some situated at intermediate points between the hypothalamus and the cortex. But a multiplicity of other factors is also involved. The schema of Mayer [2] in Figure 15 suggests the variety and complexity of the physiologic and psychological factors that may lead to overeating.

The fact that emotions have a strong influence on the appetite has long been known. While tension sometimes depresses the appetite, the majority of Freed's 500 obese patients reported that they ate more when nervous or worried, or when "idle, bored or tired." [3] This natural tendency to "comfort" oneself with good food and drink, added to such factors as the lessening need or desire for physical activity, presumably contributes most to the "creeping" obesity so often seen in the middle-aged American.

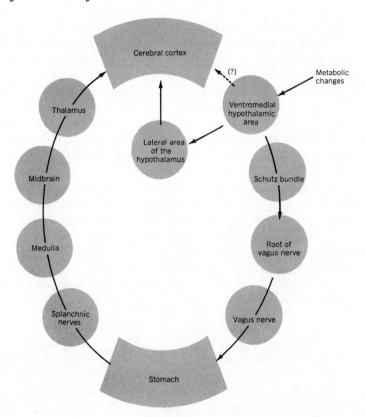

Fig. 14. An integrated view of the mechanism of the regulation of food intake.[2]

The Compulsive Eater

The grossly obese person, however, does more than simply over-eat. In most cases, he is a compulsive eater whose "addiction" to food is quite similar to the alcoholic's addiction to liquor.[4,5] For a variety of reasons, he has learned to use the eating process "to allay anxiety or to gratify pleasure cravings which should be satisfied in other ways." [4] Conrad [6] points out that the obese are "oral" people and that the activities of their mouths serve an important function for them. Moreover, food obviously has more meaning to them than to the average person. It represents health, pleasure, security and, in some cases, as many psychoanalytically oriented physicians have noted, even affection. In Bruch and Touraine's [7] study of obese children, they observed that the mothers of such children appeared to compensate for their fundamental rejection of overprotection and excessive feeding as though, unable to give their youngsters love and emotional sustenance, they could at least give them food.

Dieting not only curtails the oral function, but denies the patient the solace of food. "The reason obese patients complain of fatigue, irritability, depression and tremulousness when they start dieting is understandable," Conrad remarks.[6] "These symptoms result from anxiety which they can no longer relieve by overeating. It is during these periods of anxiety, for which they have a low tolerance, that patients frequently go off their diets." Dieting or not, the obese individual has ample reason for frequent periods of anxiety, if for no other reason than that his condition arouses so much reproach, is treated by others with so much ridicule, and is so painfully conspicuous. More than one patient has complained to Bruch, "If I only suffered from something that did not show; if there were one moment of relief when I would not be reminded of being ugly and greedy." [1]

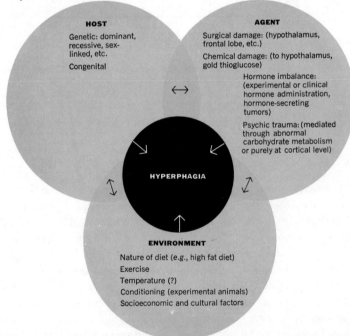

Fig. 15. A schematic view of constitutional (genetic and congenital), traumatic and environmental factors in the etiology of obesity.[2]

The fact that anxiety becomes harder to cope with when the individual is alone may explain what Stunkard [8] has termed the "Night-Eating Syndrome." He observed that 20 out of 25 obese women who were unable to follow their prescribed diets ate very little during the day, but then ate continuously from dinner on and late into the night. They felt tense and lonely and could not fall asleep without eating. "The pattern occurred during periods of life stress," he noted, "and its presence was associated with a high incidence of complications of weight-reducing regimens."

The Advantages of Being Overweight

Aside from using food to combat anxiety and loneliness, the compulsive eater also appears to have definite, if subconscious, reasons for remaining heavy. Although he may consciously wish to lose weight, he may, at the same time: [6]

1. *Associate obesity with good health.* Even patients intelligent enough to know better may subconsciously remember the parental warning, "If you don't eat, you'll get sick!" and therefore associate good health with a large and robust frame. The feeling of "weakness" that sometimes accompanies dieting may magnify the hidden fear that "illness strikes a thin, underfed person."

2. *Use obesity to bolster emotional insecurity.* The huge, shapeless body the patient professes to hate may actually represent to him a strength and power that counteract his basic feelings of weakness and insignificance. As Bruch has noted, "the large physical size provides at least a symbolic semblance of being big and strong." [9]

3. *Fear becoming attractive.* For both men and women, there may be dangers in becoming more attractive to the opposite sex and thus having to form serious emotional attachments. Too, some obese women may fear that they will lose the love of mother, sister or friend if they become more attractive and therefore more competitive.

4. *Enjoy being dependent.* As with any handicap, excess weight can be used to win the sympathy, help and protection of others. By remaining handicapped, the obese individual does not have to compete on an equal basis with other people for jobs or for love, but has a built-in excuse for being a failure.

5. *Strike back at his parents.* Particularly in children and adolescents, obesity can be an expression of hostility toward a parent. Since the obese person tends to be passive and to have difficulty expressing anger and resentment, remaining a "disgrace to the family" may be his one sure-fire means of retaliation for real or fancied injustices.

6. *Punish himself.* Obesity is, of course, a two-edged weapon, and the patient may very well be punishing himself, as well as his parents, for his hostile thoughts, his unattractive appearance, and his general feelings of worthlessness.

Dieting and Its Difficulties

For these reasons—to say nothing of the added discomfort produced by acute hunger—dieting frequently results in such highly
unpleasant symptoms as weakness, "nervousness," irritability and
fatigue, and the patient in the majority of cases soon gives up the
effort. The Gannett Clinic reports that it is successful only in about
25% of its cases—discouraging results, but as good as "if not better
than similar reports in the literature." [10] But if "simple obesity" is
extremely difficult to treat, successful weight reduction is possible,
Young observes, if the patient is reasonably well adjusted emotionally and has a meaningful reason for losing weight, and if the therapist can offer "unjudging, unchastizing, nonthreatening, sympathetic
support with sound dietary advice." [10]

Young suggests placing obese patients in three general groups,
according to the patients' apparent degree of emotional stability. In
Group 1 would be those with poor food habits and little knowledge
of food values, but who are quite stable emotionally. Group 2 would
consist of individuals with superficial emotional problems such as
anxiety, tension, and insecurity, who tend to overeat in order to
allay anxiety; these patients need emotional support, insight into
their uses of food, plus a satisfying diet. Group 3 would be composed of those with deeper emotional problems: many in this group
will not be able to reduce, and since "overeating may be the most
satisfactory way such patients have of meeting life situations," this
inability may actually be in their best interest. "Only the patient for
whom there is some likelihood of success and for whom undesirable
sequelae are not likely to follow should be encouraged to undertake
weight reduction," the nutritionist advises.[10]

Practical Therapeutic Suggestions

For "suitable" patients, Young and other investigators [1, 11] offer
additional practical suggestions. The physician should not take a
punitive approach or overemphasize the dangers of continued obesity: "In many cases we are dealing with people who are already
overanxious and they are not going to come back to someone who
makes them still more anxious." [10] It is equally wrong to stress the
rewards of successful dieting. Many obese individuals already have
badly distorted ideas of the "wonderful life" that they will lead just
as soon as they lose weight, and frequently they are bitterly disap-
pointed when the fantasied rewards do not appear. It would be

well, in fact, to discover at the outset how the patient hopes to profit from weight reduction and to be sure his motivation is sufficiently strong to help him overcome the probable unpleasantness of the first few months. The physician should try to see the patient at least once a week to discuss problems as they arise and to offer continuing reassurance and encouragement.

The prescribed diet should be individually adapted to the patient's normal food habits, his rate of energy expenditure and desired rate of weight loss. And, "despite the enthusiasm of both patient and physician for removing excess weight quickly," a diet too low in calories is not recommended. A loss of 2 pounds a week is reasonable for most adult patients, which can mean a reduction of 1,000 calories from the usual daily intake. However, proper daily caloric intake should be recommended. "A 1,000 calorie diet for all patients is absurd," Mayer asserts.[11] Mild exercise should definitely be encouraged.

Presently available pharmaceuticals may be useful adjuvants to a carefully controlled diet.[12] Of these, the amphetamines are most often administered to serve as an anorexiant and to counteract the mild depression often associated with hyperphagia. And the reports of two recent investigators [13,14] suggest that the addition of a non-depressing antianxiety agent significantly increases the percentage of successful weight-reduction programs. Such therapy "counteracts the central stimulating action of the amphetamine, and it relieves the anxiety and tension so often present in the obese, either as a causal factor, or resulting from the rigors of disciplinary reducing regimens." [13]

CHAPTER 8 BIBLIOGRAPHY

1. Bruch, H.: The Importance of Overweight, New York, Norton, 1957.
2. Mayer, J.: Postgrad Med 25:623, 1959.
3. Freed, S. C.: JAMA 133:369, 1947.
4. Weiss, E., and English, O. S.: Psychosomatic Medicine, ed 3, Philadelphia, Saunders, 1957.
5. Hamburger, W. B.: Med Clin N Amer 35:483, 1951.
6. Conrad, S. W.: J Amer Diet Ass 30:581, 1954.
7. Bruch, H., and Touraine, G.: Psychosom Med 2:141, 1940.
8. Stunkard, A. J.: Amer J Med Sci 23:77, 1957.
9. Bruch, H.: Quart J Child Behavior 3:350, 1951.
10. Young, C. M.: JAMA 185:41, 1963.
11. Mayer, J.: Postgrad Med 25:739, 1963.
12. Modell, W.: JAMA 173:1131, 1960.
13. Matlin, E.: Clin Med 70:780, 1963.
14. Settel, E.: Clin Med 70:1077, 1963.

ANXIETY AND LEARNING

A DAPTIVE FAILURE and the outbreak of a neurosis are more common in connection with starting school or failing to adjust to school than at any other time in the life of the child."[1] "Could do better" is a familiar phrase, encountered each year on the school reports of many of our children. In the past there was a handy word to explain the poor performance of such underachievers, although it suggested little in the way of a constructive course of action: "laziness."

Today's approach to the problem is more fruitful. It looks at the personality of the underachiever, at the emotional factors that basically influence the use of his intelligence and native endowment, and at the learning process itself. After an era that demanded of almost every child conformity with others of his age, we are today "aware that each child has his own capacities, assets and liabilities, all of which are in a tremendous and wonderful state of flux."[2]

And, while the new approach does not entirely dismiss the child's normal apprehensions concerning approval or punishment from parents or teachers, which guide him in his search for acceptance and love, it does give fuller recognition to the innumerable subtle expressions and influences of the detrimental effects of undue anxiety. These effects often permeate some of the children's educational and classroom experiences[3] and may cripple or interfere with their intellectual functioning.

To the physician, whom the parents expect to give counsel on all phases of their child's development, learning difficulties in children have long been a major concern. As he assesses the emotional and intellectual functioning of a child, he will often see learning difficulties as an obvious part of a more extensive psychological problem.[4] At other times, he may face the task of differentiating between pathologic anxiety, which is intellectually crippling and prevents the child from applying himself to his work, and normal anxiety, which acts as a needed incentive. And, finally, he may have to recognize the particular character of anxieties that are a consequence—not the cause—of school failure.[4]

Anxiety and Problem Solving

From many sources, it is clear that there is a characteristic lowering of intellectual control, attention and concentration in overly anxious individuals. In studies designed to elucidate the relationship of anxiety to the performance of problem-solving, as well as to basic IQ, Sarason and his group applied a variety of tests (including figure drawing, Rorschach, learning studies and others) to elementary school children.[5] The interference of high anxiety, which they noted, appeared at all levels of intelligence. And the child "who scored high on the anxiety scales manifested greater interference in problem-solving than his peer who scored low *despite the fact that both scored the same on an intelligence test.*"

Typical reading disabilities, in some cases traceable to a variety of physical factors, can also result from emotional problems.[6] According to Rabinovitch, "In order to acquire academic learning most effectively, the child must participate actively and must be free to invest appropriate psychic energy in his schooling experience. It is evident that emotional problems of any type may impair this freedom, and they therefore represent the underlying cause of learning difficulties."[7]

The reasons can be manifold.[7-8] Faced with conflicts outside the school, many children are so preoccupied in the classroom that attention and memory suffer to a point where learning is impaired. Their inner conflicts can be energy-absorbing, cause insomnia and daydreaming, and may interfere with their ability to concentrate. Depressive reactions may lead to inertia and an inability to sustain interest. In the growing youngster, worry about precocious or delayed sexual development, about actual or imaginary parental rejection, parental discord, frustrating competition with academically superior siblings—to mention just a few problems—can seriously affect emotional well-being and academic performance.

Self-Centered/Task-Centered

The effect of anxiety and tension in reducing learning efficiency has been demonstrated both in situations of experimentally induced stress and in anxiety induced by unspecified sources.[9] Diethelm and Jones found that, for most of their adult subjects, the presence of clinical anxiety significantly decreased scores on the Koh Block Design Test—which examines the patient's ability for discovering patterns, analyzing form and, generally, perceiving the relation of the whole to the part. These observers also noted that maze learning was consistently slower under anxiety conditions.[10]

The action of neurotic anxiety on learning is explained by Malmo and Amsel as forgetfulness "due to anxiety-produced interference between the relevant responses and the irrelevant responses generated out of the patient's anxiety-state." [11] In a series of experiments designed to investigate the influence of anxiety on inductive reasoning in psychoneurotic and psychopathic patients, Welch and Diethelm [12] found that "In all cases of failures anxiety was present"—but that, on the other hand, presence of anxiety does not necessarily affect reasoning in *all* patients. In those so affected, however, release from anxiety may bring improvement in reasoning. These experimenters found that 22 "failure" patients, retested after anxiety had subsided, performed under these circumstances without failure. "Anxiety may prevent psychotherapeutic progress because of its adverse influence on reasoning." [12] Two examples from this series of tests are given in Figure 16.

While these tests compare the performance of the same patients in two different moods (anxious and calm), still other tests compare the performance of two groups of patients (one of high anxiety, the

Which one of those—horse, banana, bus—would make this light go on?

Fig. 16. Under the influence of anxiety, psychopathologic patients were unable to solve these and similar written inductive-reasoning problems, although they could solve them when anxiety-free. Stirred up by anxiety, clinical signs were vagueness, rambling and inadequate definitions, all tending to "give the impression of inadequate general intelligence."
Left: Subject is asked to determine the causal factor (presence of a member of the animal class) that lights a bulb in two rows but not in a third. *Right:* The same type of problem is posed by pictures on cards, and also, in increasingly complex form, in written tests. (Adapted from Welch, L., and Diethelm, O.[12])

other of low anxiety). The experiment was carried out with college sophomores and juniors, selected and classified on the basis of an anxiety questionnaire. The results are illustrated in Figure 17. In essence, it shows a. the mean time scores of the low-anxiety group are better than those of the high-anxiety group (Fig. 17); b. the variability of the high-anxiety group is significantly larger than that of the low-anxiety group (Fig. 17). Still other findings, not shown here, suggested that c. as the learning process proceeded, the high-anxiety group tended to improve performance scores; d. an intervening report (success or failure) elicited improved performance in the low-anxiety group but depressed scores for the high-anxiety group.[13]

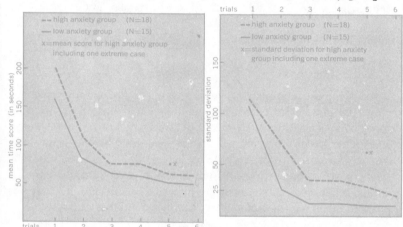

Fig. 17. Performance curve and standard deviations for high-anxiety and low-anxiety groups for 6 trials of first Koh's Block Design. Higher mean time scores (poorer performance) and greater variability in the high-anxiety groups is ascribed to feelings of inadequacy, helplessness, heightened somatic reaction, anticipations of punishment or loss of status and esteem—all self-centered rather than task-centered, reactions.

Left: Performance curve for high- and low-anxiety groups. *Right:* Standard deviations for high- and low-anxiety groups. (Adapted from Mandler, G., and Sarason, S. B.[13])

Patterns of School Failure

When learning is blocked by emotional difficulties, the pattern of errors or inabilities is often baffling. A child, for instance, may do difficult problems but miss easy ones; the problem he solved yesterday he cannot even understand today, but may tomorrow. Often, although he has learned and assimilated the material at hand, anxiety will interfere with his performance at the critical moment. "A special case of this situation is so-called test anxiety or examination panic in which the mind 'goes blank' at the sight of a test or upon being called on to speak." [14] Indeed, anxiety can be so important a variable in test performance that it has been questioned whether intelligence test scores adequately indicate the underlying abilities of individuals who have a high anxiety drive in testing situations.[13] In itself, the failure to progress in school can be a stress that, in turn, causes other emotional problems.[4] If this situation persists, the added failure at school will produce further emotional disturbance with still less ability to concentrate. The child, unable to comprehend what is being taught, is ashamed to display his ignorance in the classroom and so remains away. A vicious circle results, the child falling further behind and staying away more and more.[15]

School Phobia

What family physician or pediatrician has not been confronted with "the child who experiences nausea, abdominal pain, or non-specific malaise recurrently on school mornings, but rarely on weekends? Physical examination reveals an apparently healthy child, and recovery occurs with gratifying rapidity once the hour for school is safely past." [16] Occurring with or without psychophysiologic disorders, school phobia is a neurotic behavior manifestation [8] that appears to be increasing in incidence and has a number of causes.[7]

In certain children, school phobia is due to fear of an overstrict or overcritical teacher, a school bully or a threatening gang; in others it may be caused by school failure and the attending discouragement and loss of self-confidence. In the majority of cases, however, the fear of going to school is based on separation anxiety from the mother.[15] This anxiety, mounting even to panic, is a constant symptom, frequently accompanied by other fears of animals, toilets, strangers, sex and so on.[15] The degree of anxiety present is revealed in the surprisingly violent scene these ordinarily overly good children make when their attendance in school is enforced.[4] In fact, from the transient "Tom Sawyer" type of school morning sickness to the manifestation of a rather serious character disorder, when it occurs in the adolescent, school phobia runs a broad gamut of severity.

The therapeutic approach to school phobia consists of two phases: first, an immediate attempt to return the child to school, because the longer he stays out the more difficulty he will have in returning; and second, treatment of the underlying problem.[8] The latter often involves guidance for the parents as well—particularly for the over-protective, overanxious, possessive mother who can be regarded as an integral part of the clinical picture. Dr. Eisenberg says of such a typical case of school phobia: "The umbilical cord evidently pulled at both ends!" [17]

Readiness for School

"Doctor, do you think he's ready for school?" This is a question frequently put to the physician by anxious parents. The answer, of

Fig. 18. Goodenough "Draw-A-Man" test drawings produced by a group of children, chronologically ready for school. The observers consider the test as an index of emotional and physical maturity and as a useful predictor of school readiness. (Adapted from Coleman, J.M., Iscoc, I., and Brodsky, M. [18])

course, depends to a large extent on the child's emotional and
mental development, in addition to his physical status. The considerable diversity in the emotional and mental readiness of children—
all of them *chronologically* ready for school—is shown by Goodenough "Draw-A-Man" tests (Fig. 18) from the Children's Medical
Center, Austin, Texas.[18] Among the drawings singled out by the
observers for special comment are two whose descriptive captions
(Fig. 19) point specifically to the interaction of emotional difficulties and problems of mental development.

Fig. 19. The performance of two children. *Left:* Very largely dependent and fearful child considered for private school at age 5
years 9 months. Poor production made this inadvisable. Developed
well during next year, and at age 6 years 9 months mental age
approximated 6 years, permitting satisfaction in school situation.
   Right: This child, delayed in all phases of development, was
entered by the parents in a private school despite advice against it.
He became completely unmanageable, cried incessantly, complained of abdominal pains, though all laboratory studies were
essentially normal.

Emotional Freedom to Learn

Society's increasing recognition of the need for emotional and
mental assistance to school children, and the multifaceted aspects of
the problem—psychological, sociological and educational—raise the
question for the physician:"What is my role in such a program?"

Obviously, if the child decompensates at home only (while able to
contain himself at school),[1] the parents will turn to the physician
for help. But beyond, any emotional problem that underlies learning
difficulties—whether manifest at home or in school—is in the do-
main of medical attention and judgment. In some cases, no more
than a "common sense" approach and the passing of time will be

required.[19] In other cases, particularly of puzzling school failure, persisting school phobia, or outright truancy, the problems may be more deep-seated. While referral for psychotherapy may be desirable, it is often not practicable because of location, expense or parental reluctance. In addition to this consideration, the family doctor may often be in the best position to treat the problem because of his familiarity with the child and his parents.

Calming drugs have been used with good success in diminishing or abolishing the disruptive effects of anxiety on learning. As an anxiety neurosis yields to tranquilizing management, children's concentration, attention span, and adjustment in school improve. Similarly, as a tranquilizer relieves their separation anxiety, children with school phobia are frequently able to let go of their mothers more easily and return to school.

Finally, when the problem involves a variety of social factors as well, the physician, through his close acquaintance with the child, his family, and their environment, is in the pivotal position to evaluate the situation and to prepare and motivate the family for remedial measures.

Learning the Lessons of Life

School, of course, is hardly the only source for man's learning. Life itself can be an even more exacting taskmaster. From his infant years through maturity, man grapples with situations of stress and anxiety as he learns the difficult lessons of life.

Erikson [20] suggests eight such learning periods, each with its emotional crisis to be resolved before the individual can move satisfactorily to the next level. They are:

1. Infants—learning *trust vs. mistrust*
2. Very young children—learning *autonomy vs. shame*
3. Preschool children—learning *initiative vs. guilt*
4. School-age children—learning *industry vs. inferiority*
5. Adolescents—learning *identity vs. identity confusion*
6. Young adults—learning *intimacy vs. isolation*
7. Productive adults—learning *generativity vs. self-absorption*
8. Mature adults—learning *personality integration vs. despair.*

CHAPTER 9 BIBLIOGRAPHY

1. Cramer, J. B.: *in* Arieti, S., ed.: American Handbook of Psychiatry, vol 1, New York, Basic, 1959, p. 808.

2. Mezer, R. R.: Dynamic Psychiatry in Simple Terms, ed 2, New York, Springer Pub Co, 1960, pp. 151 ff.
3. May, R.: The Meaning of Anxiety, New York, Ronald Press, 1950, p. 15.
4. Hofling, C. K.: Textbook of Psychiatry for Medical Practice, Philadelphia, Lippincott, 1963, pp. 533 ff.
5. Sarason, S. B., *et. al.:* Anxiety in Elementary School Children, New York, Wiley, 1960, pp. 159 ff., 187 ff.
6. Reed, J. C., and Auld, F., Jr.: *in* Deutsch, A., and Fishman, H., eds.: The Encyclopedia of Mental Health, vol 3, New York, The Encyclopedia of Mental Health, A Division of Franklin Watts, Inc., 1963, p. 943.
7. Rabinovitch, R. D.: *in* Arieti, S., ed.: *op. cit.,* vol 1, pp. 860 ff.
8. Glaser, K., and Clemmens, R. L.: Pediatrics *35:*128, 1965.
9. Feldhusen, J. F., and Klausmeier, H. J.: Child Develop *33:*403, 1962.
10. Diethelm, O., and Jones, M. R.: Arch Neurol & Psychiat *58:*325, 1947.
11. Malmo, R. B., and Amsel, A.: J Exper Psychol *38:*440, 1948.
12. Welch, L., and Diethelm, O.: Arch Neurol & Psychiat *63:*87, 1950.
13. Mandler, G., and Sarason, S. B.: J Abnorm Psychol *47:*166, 1952.
14. Wattenberg, W. W.: *in* Deutsch, A., and Fishman, H., eds.: *op. cit.,* vol 5, pp. 1803 ff.
15. Bakwin, H., and Bakwin, R. M.: Clinical Management of Behavior Disorders in Children, ed 2, Philadelphia, Saunders, 1960, pp. 311 ff., 318 ff.
16. Eisenberg, L.: Pediat Clin N Amer *5:*645, 1958.
17. ———: Amer J Psychiat *114:*712, 1958.
18. Coleman, J. M., Iscoe, I., and Brodsky, M.: Pediatrics *24:*275, 1959.
19. Bakwin, H.: Pediat Clin N Amer *5:*559, 1958.
20. Richmond, J. B., and Hersher, L.: *in* Deutsch, A., and Fishman, H., eds.: *op. cit.,* vol 1, pp. 292 ff.; and Erikson, E. H.: *in* Stein, M. R., Vidick, A. J., and White, D. M., eds.: Identity and Anxiety, Glencoe (Ill), Free Press, 1960, p. 52.

ANXIETY AND SPEECH DISORDERS

I N PRIMEVAL TIMES, when "the creatures began to live in groups, the vocal cords were developed so that they could warn one another of danger, attract one another, express their rage and anger, and so escape being overwhelmed or destroyed. Human speech was evolved out of these first primitive cries and calls and songs." [2]

Your Speech Reveals Your Personality [1]

Ever since, human speech has remained primarily a means of expressing emotions.[2] True, animals possess certain means of emotional and directive communications: for instance, birds, employ a variety of signs and sounds for indicating danger or sexual situations; bees possess a sign language by which they can indicate to their fellows the type, direction and approximate distance of food.[3] But these simple, direct communications are of an entirely different quality from the intricate system of symbols and meanings man employs competently as language. "If there is any one capability that is uniquely human," finds Wooldridge, "it is the power of speech" [3]—human because possessed by man only and unique because it serves as a subtle mirror of his personality, his most intimate thoughts and emotions, his frailties and fortitudes.

Physiology of Speech Is Complex

The highly discriminating faculty of speech is served by "the human's most complex and finely balanced muscular activity." [4] And it is precisely because of the numerous nerve areas and muscle groups requiring perfect coordination and harmony that speech is so susceptible to disorganization during periods of emotional tension and self-consciousness.[4,5] "At such times, the lines of communication are thrown out of gear, the nerve messages go astray, and

71

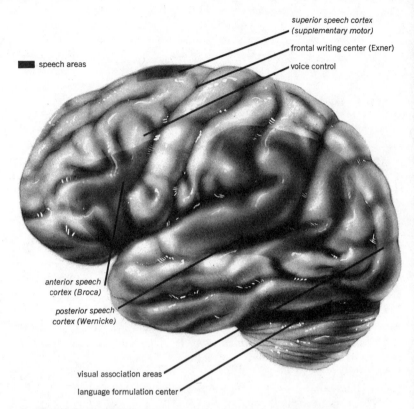

Fig. 20. The three areas of the human cerebral cortex instrumental in the ideational elaboration of speech. Motor mechanisms of speech, including voice control, articulating movements, and vocalization, lie in the supplementary motor areas of either side, situated close to and between the principal areas of ideational speech. (Adapted from Penfield, W., and Roberts, L.[7]; and Ulett, G. A., and Goodrich, D. W.[8])

we find distortions and definite emotional disturbances in the area of verbalization." [4]

Localization of the cortical regions involved in speech has proved a difficult task: the fact that man is the only animal with articulate speech has precluded animal experimentation.[6] Some of the results of our still incomplete understanding of the ideational areas of speech in the cerebral cortex are given in Figure 20. On the basis of Penfield's experiments, it is now assumed that all speech areas, ordinarily, are situated in the left hemisphere—not, as held by earlier beliefs, in the dominant hemisphere (defined by left- or righthandedness).[3, 7, 8] From Penfield's studies it also seems likely that extensive damage in the uppermost speech area may result in transfer of its function to adjacent areas of the cortex and to the two remaining speech areas.[3, 7]

This "redundancy" has raised the question of how the three separate speech areas are connected. After numerous operations on different patients, Penfield reasoned that these areas must interconnect through the brainstem. Anatomical dissection shows, in fact, dense fiber tracts leading from each of the cortical speech areas to the posterior part of the thalamus, at the top of the brainstem.[3, 7] Such a speech-integrating role of the brainstem would agree with the wider concept of the cortex as an organ of elaboration and refinement of function, which is basically controlled by the phylogenetically older parts of the brain.[3]

Speech in the Making

An infant's first action immediately after birth is to cry.[9] Crying continues as its only mode of vocal functioning during the first few months, then is followed by a stage of babbling and finally by the beginning of verbal symbolization.[9] At this stage, "if a particular sound is met with the reward of tenderness, it will be reiterated," [10] and may, from a repeatable noise, advance to a symbolizing word. "Once he masters a few of these simple symbols he is said to be talking." [11] For the child just emerging from helpless infancy, speech is the chief means of adjusting to the group in an adult way.[2] The speech faculty develops his ego functions and consolidates his consciousness.[12] From here on, "his linguistic attainments progress with astounding speeds. At 18 months, he knows only a few single words. In the next three years, he acquires several thousand words, combines them into sentences, and learns to tell his wishes, experiences, feelings, and deductions." [9]

The chronology of the normal development of speech in the child is shown in Tables 3 and 4. To the extent to which the child fails to keep the time schedule of Table 3, his language development may be considered abnormal. His speech also is retarded if there are abnormalities in sound, syllable and word patterns.[13] Problems of speech and language in the child can be conveniently grouped [9]:

absence of speech—mutism
delayed onset of speech
disorders of articulation
disorders of phonation

disorders of rhythm—stuttering
disorders of comprehension
disorders of symbolization.

TABLE 3. *Normal development of language in the child.* (Adapted from Duffy, J. K., and Irwin, J. V.[15])

Age in years	1	1½	2	3	3½	4	4½	5	5½	6½	7½
Appearance of individual sounds *					[m], [b], [p], [h], [w]. All vowels of English		[k], [g], [t], [d], [n], [ŋ] (ng), [j] (y)		[i]	[v], [j] (sh), [ʒ] (zh), [l], [ð] (th)	[s], [z], [r], [hw] (wh), [θ] (th), [tʃ] (ch), [dʒ] (i)
Size of vocabulary (in words)	1	20-100	200-300	900		1500					
Word type (in order of most common use)	nouns	nouns, some verbs and other parts	nouns, verbs, and other parts	verbs, nouns, pronouns, adjectives		verbs, pronouns, nouns					
Sentence length		1 word	2 words	3 words							
Intelligibility of child's speech		25%	66%	90%				100%			

* The indicated age represents the upper limit of normality. Any sound may appear, and frequently does, before the age indicated.

TABLE 4. *Development of sounds in the infant appears to follow a definite pattern. Initially, various sounds produced are related to the infant's physiologic state. Then control develops, usually in the stages shown at left.* (Adapted from Krech, D., and Crutchfield, R. S.[14])

CONTROL OF	DURING MONTHS OF LIFE
volume	2nd
pitch	3rd or 4th
sequence	5th

While their etiologies range from auditory or neurologic disorders to malformations of the speech-forming organs, an emotional component can be found in most of these problems. This correlation of speech difficulties with emotional factors is perhaps best exemplified by the stutterer.

The Mystery of Stuttering

About 1,300,000 Americans are stutterers, roughly half of them children. The affliction is no respecter of social or economic status; it is found among all races, all levels of intelligence, and its occurrence can be traced to antiquity (see Fig. 21).[4] One ill-explained differ-

Aesop   *Demosthenes*   *Aristotle*   *Virgil*   *Erasmus*

Lamb   *King George VI*   *Churchill*   *Maugham*

Fig. 21. Famous persons afflicted with stuttering.

ence is that of sex: stuttering is decidedly more frequent and persistent in boys than in girls; the reported ratios vary from 2:1 to 10:1; adult female stutterers are rare.[9] Confusion also prevails with regard to its etiology. Stuttering, says Barbara, has properly been

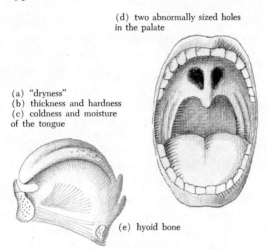

(d) two abnormally sized holes
in the palate

(a) "dryness"
(b) thickness and hardness
(c) coldness and moisture
of the tongue

(e) hyoid bone

Fig. 22. Historical theories on the etiology of stuttering as held by *a.* Hippocrates, *b.* Aristotle, *c.* Francis Lord Bacon, *d.* Santorini, and *e.* Morgagni.[4]

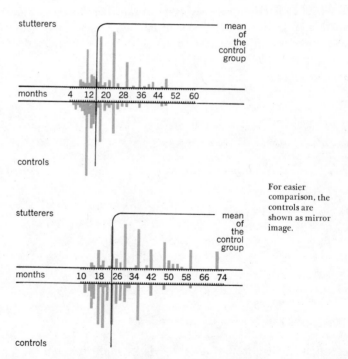

For easier comparison, the controls are shown as mirror image.

Fig. 23. Age in months of onset of speech (*top*) and of development of intelligible speech (*bottom*) in stutterers and nonstutterers. (Adapted from Berry, M. F.[16])

called "the disorder of many theories."[4] Approaches in former times frequently centered on an abnormality of the tongue as the basis for defective speech (see Fig. 22). By the middle of the nineteenth century, tongue surgery was still practiced as a remedial means for stuttering. And even today, the idea that tongue-tie causes stuttering is prevalent among the laity.[9]

In our time, stutterers have been subjected to every conceivable examination in physiology and biochemistry—with few findings that are enlightening.[9] There seems some predisposition in stutterers to an original motor disorganization, since stuttering children appear to be more awkward at acquiring motor skills.[4] Evidence suggesting that stuttering may be inherited is apparent in the developmental history of stutterers: Berry found that stuttering children began to speak later and became intelligible in their speech later than non-stuttering children [16] (see Fig. 23). But in spite of the search for factors of an anatomical, physiological, neurological and biochemical nature, an organic basis for stuttering has yet to be established.[17] The majority of today's speech therapists and psychiatrists have shifted the etiologic emphasis *to the stuttering person.* Stuttering is viewed not so much as the primary difficulty itself but "as a dynamically determined symptom of personal difficulty."[9]

The Two Stutterings

Much in the pathogenesis of stuttering supports the psychogenic approach. In 90% of the cases, the onset of the affliction occurs under the age of 10, "and the majority of these cases start in the first 5 years, when the first major social adjustments begin."[4] Two phases are usually distinguishable, a primary and a secondary one.[18] The *primary* is manifest by hesitant, loose or repetitious speech.[4,9] Rather than stuttering, this may be more correctly called "nonfluency."[19] After all, the child is not always trying to communicate the way adults do. For one thing, children love to repeat syllables and to say things like "pinky panky poo" or "hickory dickory dock"; indeed from 15% to 20% of their words figure in such repetitions.[5] For another, when, with a limited vocabulary, the child tries to express thoughts, feelings, eagerness or excitement in words, he inevitably runs into a "speech block—a sort of road block in verbal thinking."[19] But it is at this point that tense parents "who are perfectionists will often find this hesitancy alarming and will tag it as a stutter."[4]

Outgrowth of Normal Nonfluency?

Made aware of his primary symptoms, the child may now develop *secondary* ones.[18] He may enter into what is known as "secondary blocking," passing from the phase of simple repetitive speech to forcing and struggling with his speech attempts. While previously unaware of an affliction, the mere thought of speaking now terrifies him.[4] The parents, in turn, growing more anxious, hector the child to "go slowly," "stop and start over," "make up your mind" or "breathe more deeply." In the end, a vicious spiral is set up wherein the child, ever more fearful and disheartened, speaks ever more laboriously and frantically. Thus an initial groping for words or "normal nonfluency," through the tensions of parental and other environmental disapproval may assume in certain cases, the abnormal qualities of real stuttering.[20-21]

But in addition to parental coerciveness, since stuttering develops when speech is not yet organized into a secure and dependable function of the personality, stuttering may be precipitated by almost any experience that, in an emotionally insecure child, generates anxiety and fear. Such disorganizing stresses are of two kinds—acute-sudden and continuing. The acute traumatic experiences are more easily identified—"a fall, a flood, a fire, an illness, a surgical operation, an automobile accident, bereavement, etc." [19] or forcible conversion from left- to righthandedness.[4] The continuing stresses are less obviously pinpointed—a worrisome home environment, an overbearing father, a nagging, possessive mother, a bullying brother, a domineering sister, to name a few.[4,19] School, with its competitive atmosphere, may further cripple the stutterer's personality, making him feel something of an oddity, inferior to other children.

Who Would Marry a Stutterer?

In fact, for the stutterer of any age, the most disturbed emotional area is perhaps that of self-conceptualization [22] (see Fig. 24). Because in our culture stuttering is regarded as a deficiency and a blemish, the stutterer builds "a self-concept that includes inferiority and guilt as central characteristics." [23] "He possesses many fears, seems burdened with a marked sense of guilt, and feels inadequate as a person." In the sexual area, stutterers appear to experience the same inhibitive, hostile feelings that also interfere with fluent speech. The predominant feeling is one of inadequacy, rationalized by such statements as "What girl would want to marry a stutterer,

Fig. 24. Changes in the disturbed self-concept of stutterers under-going psychotherapy are revealed in their progressive self-drawings. (Adapted from Clark, R. M., and Fitzpatrick, J. A.[24])

Top: Annie, 8½ years, presenting secondary stuttering with clonic and tonic blocks. At age 5, she had been diagnosed as mentally retarded from organic causes, with secondary neurotic reactions. *a.* Drawn prior to therapy; the wide-eyed startled expression reflects Annie's grimaces during gasping blocks; *b.* following 2 months of therapeutic sessions designed to provide outlet for her emotional tensions and anxieties, her stuttering has improved to "dysfluency"; *c.* after 3 months of therapy, the final drawing shows a happier, "freer," more mobile child. A change in self-concept is manifest.

Bottom: George, 23 years, presenting severe stuttering, the blocks accompanied by marked facial contortions. *a.* At onset of group therapy, his self-portrayal reveals exasperation and defeat; the face is given an infantile representation while the "blowing of his top" portrays the internal pressure experienced during blocks; the ears are nonhearing and the eyes are nonseeing; *b.* after 30 group therapeutic sessions, the final drawing depicts a freer, less tense face, its configuration more natural, more like his own.

anyway?" or "I am afraid that if I have children, they'd stutter, too."[22] The stutterer generally seeks solitary, nonverbal roles both for pleasure and vocation.[23] Children may go so far as to hide when visitors come to the home.[9] In constant dread of being defeated as he speaks, the stutterer avoids difficult words and menacing situations. Obsessive in his attitudes toward his speech difficulties, "he lives his anxieties in retrospect and in anticipation." [19]

Stuttering not only blocks speech but, by disturbing the emotions, often also impedes clear thinking.[2] Before attempting to speak, the stutterer procrastinates and anxiously thinks about what he will say, how he will say it, and when. He is beset by self-doubts and indecisiveness. The tremendous expenditure of energy implicit in an ordeal of this sort leaves him frustrated, hopelessly resigned and exhausted. Typically, he is a chronic hesitator in other areas of life.[4]

Examining the Stream of Talk

Beyond such an obvious disruption of fluent speech as stuttering, there are many other modifications in emotion-linked speech. When first viewing a patient, in fact, a psychiatric examiner "views his stream of speech in general terms, amount, speed, pressure, just as the internist first determines the volume, speed and pressure of the blood stream." [11] Speech may be clear and animated, the voice quiet or monotonous; the patient may converse spontaneously, reluctantly or not at all; he may answer questions relevantly, circumstantially or irrelevantly. "In the psychoneuroses and in disorders of character, personality and social behavior, the main abnormality to be found is in the content." [25]

Finally, the problem of psychological analysis of human speech

TABLE 5. *Examples of common speech disturbances* (Adapted from Mahl, G. F.[26])

CATEGORY	EXAMPLE	AVERAGE %
1. "Ah"	Well . . . ah . . . when I first came home.	40.5
2. Sentence change	That was . . . it will be 2 years ago in the fall.	25.3
3. Repetition	'Cause they . . . they get along pretty well together.	19.2
4. Stutter	It sort of well I . . . I . . . leaves a memory	7.8
5. Omission	She mour . . . was in mourning for about 2 years	4.5
6. Sentence incompletion	Well I'm sorry I couldn't get here last week so I could . . . ah . . . I was getting a child ready for camp and finishing up swimming lessons.	1.2
7. Tongue-slips	He was born in their hou(se) . . . hospital and came to their house.	0.7
8. Intruding incoherent sound	If I see a girl now I'd like to take out I just . . . dh . . . ask her.	1.2
	Total	*100.4*

may be approached by analyzing the many rather discrete hesitations and disturbances in the spontaneous flow of speech. G. F. Mahl, in studies of a group composed of psychoneurotic patients, therapists, Yale undergraduates and faculty members, found speech disturbances of this type surprisingly common. They are classified and listed (with stuttering included for better comparison) in Table 5. On the average, one of these disturbances was observed for every 16 words or every 4.6 seconds of speech.[26] Except for the "ah-category," their relationship to anxiety was evident from yet another study of 25 experimental subjects and 20 controls. In this experiment, when anxiety was manipulated by an interview setting (neutral interview A followed by stressful interview B), the increase in speech disturbances of the "non-ah" group averaged 34.2% per subject —a clearly "sizable" rate. Measurements of palmar sweat revealed positive, if modest, association with the speech disturbances.[27]

A Broad Therapeutic Field

Problems of speech and language are so manifold that the therapeutic requirements range over a wide area. In cleft palate and harelip, for instance, even after successful surgery, entrenched patterns and residual difficulties still need attention to prevent handicaps and unhappiness in later life. This may also be true of faulty enunciation and phonation (not brought about by local pathology) because of the effect they have on the patient and those around him.[*] "The stutterer's plight is especially pathetic."[9] Often his adequate management involves the cooperative treatment by both the psychotherapist and the speech pathologist. A significant dimension of stuttering requiring therapeutic attention is emotional disturbance—whether viewed as the basic cause of stuttering or its inevitable result.[23]

For the stuttering *child* not fully cognizant of his problem, the approach is mainly one of helping the parents create a home atmosphere in which speaking is made more rewarding and more fun for the child.[4, 2, 8] Speech therapy in children is considered a measure *supportive* and part of general psychotherapy.[9] The *adolescent* or *adult* stutterer is particularly affected by what others think of him. Also, he often considers his speech difficulties, rather than his emotional problems, the main impediment. "I have some emotional

___

[*] Information concerning the various speech services in the USA are available from the American Speech and Hearing Association, 1001 Connecticut Ave., NW, Washington, DC 20036.[28]

problems," runs the classical statement of such a patient, "but if I were able to overcome my speech handicap, my other problems would work themselves out." [29]

Yet in today's psychotherapeutic approach, emphasis is away from symptoms as the prime expressions of underlying disturbances and toward the treatment of the total personality, the whole man." [4] Such a total approach may meet with considerable resistance, since the adult stutterer "lives in constant dread of having his protective structures invaded or removed. He is highly sensitive to criticism and fears open discussion of himself, for he cannot face his conflicts squarely or bear their related anxiety." [30] Psychoanalytic therapy for stutterers, of course, is further complicated by the fact that speech—the objective of therapy—is also the very instrument of therapy.[12, 31] Medicinal tranquilization, by interrupting the vicious circle of tension, speech inhibition and consequent anxiety, may help restore speech confidence in the stutterer.

CHAPTER 10 BIBLIOGRAPHY

1. Barbara, D. A.: Your Speech Reveals Your Personality, Springfield (Ill), Thomas, 1958, title page.
2. Blanton, S.: in Barbara, D. A., ed.: New Directions in Stuttering, Springfield (Ill), Thomas, 1965, pp. 3 ff.
3. Wooldridge, D. E.: The Machinery of the Brain, New York, McGraw-Hill, 1963, pp. 153, 158, 161 ff.
4. Barbara, D. A.: in Arieti, S., ed.: American Handbook of Psychiatry, vol 1, New York, Basic, 1959, pp. 950 ff.
5. Alvarez, W. C.: The Neuroses, Philadelphia, Saunders, 1955, pp. 280 ff.
6. Krief, W.: Functional Neuroanatomy, New York, Blakiston, 1953, VII of insert, p. 388.
7. Penfield, W., and Roberts, L.: Speech and Brain Mechanisms, Princeton (NJ), Princeton Univ Press, 1959, pp. 92, 188, 196-198 ff.
8. Ulett, G. A., and Goodrich, D. W.: A Synopsis of Contemporary Psychiatry, ed 2, St. Louis, Mosby, 1960, pp. 42 ff.
9. Kanner, L.: Child Psychiatry, ed 3, Springfield (Ill), Thomas, 1960, pp. 509 ff.
10. Witenberg, E. G., Rioch, J. M., and Mazer, M.: in Arieti, S., ed.: op. cit., vol 2, p. 1421.
11. Ewalt, J. R., Strecker, E. A., and Ebaugh, F. G.: Practical Clinical Psychiatry, ed 8, New York, Blakiston, McGraw-Hill, 1957, pp. 11, 82.
12. Fenichel, O.: The Psychoanalytic Theory of Neurosis, New York, Norton, 1945, pp. 42, 317.
13. Berry, M. E., and Eisenson, J.: Speech Disorders, Principles and Practices of Therapy, New York, Appleton, 1956, pp. 83 ff.
14. Krech, D., and Crutchfield, R. S.: Elements of Psychology, New York, Knopf, 1959, p. 461.
15. Duffy, J. K., and Irwin, J. V.: Speech and Hearing Hurdles, Columbus (Ohio), School and College Service, 1951, p. 11.

16. Berry, M. F.: J Pediat *12*:209, 1938.

17. Johnson, W., *et al.*: Speech Handicapped School Children, rev ed, New York, Harper, 1956, p. 226.

18. Douglass, E.: Canad Med Ass J *64*:397, 1951.

19. Bluemel, C. S.: *in* Barbara, D. A., ed.: The Psychotherapy of Stuttering, Springfield (Ill), Thomas, 1962, pp. 48 ff.

20. Bloodstein, O., Alper, J. P., and Zisk, P. K.: *in* Barbara, D. A., ed.: *op. cit.*, ref. 2, p. 52.

21. Johnson, W.: Quart J Speech *30*:330, 1944.

22. Snyder, M. A.: *in* Barbara, D. A., ed.: *op. cit.*, ref. 19, pp. 42 ff.

23. Villareal, J.: *in* Barbara, D. A., ed.: *ibid.*, pp. 103 ff., 117.

24. Clark, R. M., and Fitzpatrick, J. A.: *in* Barbara, D. A., ed.: *ibid.*, pp. 166 ff., 182 ff.

25. Gregory, I.: Psychiatry, Biological and Social, Philadelphia, Saunders, 1961, pp. 42, 73.

26. Mahl, G. F.: Disturbances in the patient's speech as a function of anxiety; and "normal" disturbances in spontaneous speech as a function of anxiety. Papers read at Amer Psychol Ass Convention, 1956; and J Abnorm Soc Psychol *53*:1, 1956.

27. Kasl, S. V., and Mahl, G. F.: J Personality Soc Psychol *1*:425, 1965.

28. Johnson, W.: *in* Deutsch, A., and Fishman, H., eds.: The Encyclopedia of Mental Health, vol 6, New York, The Encyclopedia of Mental Health, A Division of Franklin Watts, Inc., 1963, pp. 1958, 1960.

29. Pellman, C.: *in* Barbara, D. A., ed.: *op. cit.*, ref. 19, p. 123.

30. Barbara, D. A., ed.: *op. cit.*, ref. 19, pp. 272 ff.

31. Ruesch, J.: *in* Arieti, S., ed.: *op. cit.*, pp. 895 ff.

EMOTIONAL PROBLEMS OF COLLEGE STUDENTS

PRACTICALLY ALL psychiatrists who have worked with college students agree that a considerable number of them are likely to need help each year because of emotional problems which interfere seriously with their work. A common estimate is 10%.[2]

Problems of the Transition

Going away to college uproots young people from their home environments and deprives them of the immediate support of their families. In these trying circumstances, they are obliged to make many new adjustments—and at a time when much more is expected of them scholastically than ever before.[3] The normal problems of growing up, encountered frequently during this stage, are usually transient and not incapacitating. More important are the deep-seated emotional disturbances that can be activated or intensified by the stresses of adapting to life away from home.[3]

For the insecure student, being "on his own" can be quite unsettling. The relaxation of discipline at the university level deprives him of familiar reassuring controls.[4] Instead of feeling free, he is likely to feel alone. Previously, work was fed to him in measurable amounts; he knew what he must learn, and he was examined frequently. In the university he finds less direction, less direct contact with his teachers and a study program so wide that he may be paralyzed by its magnitude. Unless he quickly develops a critical selective ability, he will dissipate his efforts, and can work himself into a state of exhaustion. On the other hand, lack of disciplinary pressure may mislead him into doing far less work than is necessary.[4] In either event, his new "freedom" can be a source of anxiety and may initiate difficulties which will try him throughout his college years.

The high school "celebrity" finds the transition period particularly hard. No matter how small the university or college he enters, he is bound to feel relegated to comparative anonymity. The student whose insecurity was kept at bay by academic, social or athletic prowess misses the reassurance of his former eminence.[4]

Presenting Symptoms of the Student's Reaction to Stress

The most common emotional disorders in college students, studies indicate, are the psychoneuroses.[1] The inclination is to consider these disorders transient manifestations of adolescent instability. But if the college student's attitudes and reactions are *chronically* adolescent and detrimental to his emotional, social and academic life, then he is probably ill. The essential factor—*chronicity*—is easily overlooked in dealing with what appear to be surface problems. While the emotional disturbances of students are no different from those of the general population, the presenting symptoms are unique to his situation.[1]

Apathy is one signal of emotional conflict. The apathetic student unconsciously finds dozens of ways to postpone or avoid work.[2] He sharpens pencils; he plays solitaire; he goes to the movies or visits friends. He is not particularly interested in learning *per se*, but merely in obtaining its symbol—the degree—in order to forward social or vocational goals. For him, being in college is "bad" but graduating is "good." While failure to take advantage of educational opportunities may not be particularly deleterious during the college years, it can become a problem later on in life. Then, the Now-it-is-too-late syndrome sets in, with its consequence of bitterness, frustration, and many other psychological difficulties.[5]

Isolation. Self-inflicted or imposed from without, isolation is another indication that the student is in emotional trouble. Stress may cause him to withdraw from all extracurricular activity, or to express himself in words and behavior that are incomprehensible to his friends and to himself.[2] Sometimes, the isolation is due to cultural or social differences between the family and college environments. For instance, the rural student in an urban college, or the foreign student in a strange land, often suffers from "psychological unbalance." Whether the unbalance develops into an illness depends on the student's ability to adjust to the new conditions. If he already has many neurotic difficulties, he may not be able to establish a new equilibrium.[5]

Aggression. The students who react to stress with hostility or aggression are the hardest of all to understand or to tolerate. Although friendship may be the thing they most want and need: "They act in such a way as to provoke others to dislike them, they destroy property, they use alcohol quite inappropriately, they criticize others, and in general they manage to lose most of their friends, actual or potential." [2]

Learning difficulties. No problems of emotional adjustment are more puzzling than those involving difficulties in learning. If they are related to realistic life situations—a broken engagement, serious illness in the family—supportive treatment in the form of psychotherapy is usually sufficient.[6] If the learning difficulties are associated with a repressed emotional conflict, however, then the problem is more complex. In these instances, anxiety becomes so unbearable that the student is obliged to defend himself by an inhibition toward the learning process. "The inhibition may be an acute, isolated reaction in a relatively healthy personality or it may be only one of many chronic manifestations in a total neurosis or character disorder."[6] The treatment of learning difficulties, unlike other emotional adjustment problems, is complicated by a time element. Results must be obtained in a relatively short time to prevent interruption of the student's education. It is important, therefore, to determine as quickly as possible the nature of the inhibition, so that efforts can be made to detach it from the learning situation.

Examination anxiety. Even when students know their subjects, anxiety can cause them to "blow up" during examinations. "Fear of tests seems to afflict most students and is probably an occupational disease."[7] But when examination anxiety assumes panic proportions, it usually has its origin in unresolved personal problems of long standing. The student needs support during the acute period, and in some cases it might be useful to use a psychotherapeutic agent as a temporary aid. But he should almost never be excused from the examination, and once the acute stage is over, extended psychotherapy should be instituted.[5]

Psychiatric disorders. Psychotic breakdowns occur in college students with disquieting frequency.[2] The incidence of schizophrenia among those with emotional difficulties has been estimated to be as high as 24.6%[1] Suicidal tendencies are much more common than generally assumed, and for every student who actually commits suicide, there are 50 more who are suicidally inclined.[8] These students are found to be significantly more depressed, more obsessive-compulsive and more schizoid than nonsuicidal students. Whenever this symptom pattern is observed, clinicians should be alert to the possibility of suicidal tendencies.

Recommendations

Methods should be devised to identify emotionally handicapped students early in their college careers—especially if they can benefit from individual counseling or psychotherapy. College psychiatrists believe that unsatisfactory family relationships and poor environmental conditions are important causes of emotional illness and failure in students.[2, 9] Students, however, should not be screened out because of unfavorable backgrounds. Many have overcome adverse circumstances and gone on to become our most productive citizens. Unfortunately, many more have not, and these should be salvaged, if possible.

DIAGNOSIS

The psychological disorders of students should be fully diagnosed. Too often, they are underdiagnosed, for a number of reasons. For one thing, it is difficult to accept the idea that a young patient of intellectual endowment and academic achievement can be emotionally ill. Then, too, the busy therapist in a college mental hygiene clinic must concentrate on immediate or precipitating complaints, so that underlying pathology is often overlooked.[1] "It is a constant temptation," Reik says, "to minimize emotional problems without taking the trouble to discover what they are, to say nothing of how serious they are." [10]

Adequate diagnostic and treatment facilities should not only exist in colleges and universities, they should be *known* to exist.[4] Psychiatrists have an important specialized role to play in counseling students and advising school authorities. In addition, traditional sources of help for students in distress—the older friend, the general practitioner, the trusted professor—should be part of the psychological life line. The student should feel free to approach any of them. Those in a position to help should know of each other; then referrals are easily made and problems explored. In this way, flexible informal and efficient arrangements can be made to identify and support the disturbed student, before he sinks beneath the weight of his emotional burdens.

CHAPTER 11 BIBLIOGRAPHY

1. Seltzer, M. L.: Arch Gen Psychiat (Chicago) 2:131, 1960.
2. Farnsworth, D. L.: Ment Hyg 43:351, 1959.
3. Llewellyn, C. E., Jr.: Ment Hyg 48:93, 1964.
4. Davy, B. W.: Proc Roy Soc Med 53:764, 1960.
5. Funkenstein, D. H., ed.: The Student and Mental Health, Cambridge, Riverside Press, 1956, pp. 305-306, 313-316.
6. Dunlap, K. W.: Ment Hyg 43:237, 1959.
7. Lott, G. M.: J Med Ass Georgia 52:188, 1963.
8. Braaten, L. J.: Ment Hyg 47:562, 1963.
9. Farnsworth, D. L.: Ment Hyg 43:568, 1959.
10. Reik, L. E.: Ment Hyg 39:465, 1955.

ANXIETY AND THE MALE PSYCHE

IN TODAY'S competitive society, where masculinity and even virtue are so often equated with success,[1] the American male can rarely afford to relax. To win recognition from both men and women he must be a success in his business or profession; he must advance, make money, go up fast. In addition, if possible, "he should also be likable, attractive and well groomed, a good mixer, well informed, good at the leisure-time activities of his class, should provide well for his home, keep his car in good condition, be attentive enough to his wife so that he doesn't give other women an opportunity to catch his interest." [2]

As Orr [1] has pointed out, men's goals are hard, the risks great, and the failures numerous.

Fear of Being "Unmanly"

Like women, men are under particularly heavy stress during periods of major adaptive efforts. For adult males, these typically include leaving the parental home, serving in the armed forces, marrying, becoming a father, getting ahead in business, growing older, and retiring. Men's problems, however, are compounded by an unspoken obligation to live up to society's concept of ideal masculinity. This concept requires the adult male to "act like a man" in difficult situations or actual crisis. Whatever occurs, a man must be "stronger" and "better controlled" than a woman would be. Which may be one of the reasons he dies earlier than his wife. Men—according to one point of view—"dam up their feelings and develop ulcers and high blood pressure. Women, being feminine, are irrational, complaining, given to tears—and to burying their husbands." [1]

Any real or apparent failure to live up to the masculine ideal invites loss of self-esteem, strong feelings of guilt or shame, and even depression. "It is therefore harder for a man to be sick, injured, unemployed, or in any way 'inadequate' than it is for a woman or child," Orr observes, "and therefore more productive of symptoms of emotional stress and conflict." [1]

Inadequacy and the Bachelor

An unconscious feeling of inadequacy may be one of the reasons why the confirmed bachelor—who has "failed" in one very important area of life—tends to be less happy than generally supposed. At any rate, contrary to the popular stereotypes of the "frustrated old maid" and the "free and unencumbered bachelor life," two recent studies [3,4] found that single men are less happy and more emotionally maladjusted than married men—and than single women, also.

One team of investigators [3] suggests: "Because of the greater freedom of choice men have in the marriage market, it seems likely that those among them who are either unable or unwilling to get married were more psychologically impaired to begin with." Gurin and his co-workers [4] find another distinction between single men and single women:

Women are seen as more able to form or to maintain other than marital attachments; their ties to the family and friends can be very strong. The story of the single aunt who assumes the role of a doting mother-figure to her nieces and nephews is not uncommon. For a single man, however, in addition to the stereotype stressing freedom and independence, there is also the picture of the lonely, anomic, rootless man, living out his life in single rooms. Perhaps it is in an ability to form and maintain meaningful personal attachments that we may find a clue to these differences we have seen—that single women are less distressed than single men.

Paying for Success

But even the man who lives up to the masculine ideal in every way may pay a heavy price for his striving. The exhausting struggle for success takes its inevitable toll. Many hard-driving men, for instance, find themselves with an ulcer; some, indeed, even take a certain pride in this "badge of success." And like the stomach or duodenal ulcer, cardiovascular disease is also principally an ailment of men and in many cases of men under pressure (though there is some evidence that women—particularly women executives—are beginning to catch up).[5]

Coronary disease, of course, has roots in heredity, diet, body chemistry and body mechanics, but more and more evidence is pointing to the importance of chronic emotional stress in its genesis.

The proportion of coronary thrombosis patients at the Englewood Hospital in New Jersey, Gordon notes, is almost five times as large as at rural Olean General. And, he observes, "a susceptible man who works too hard, hurries too much, relaxes too little and sleeps badly, who is chronically tense and fearful and who often goes through periods of acute worry" is a likely candidate for a cardiac problem.[5]

The study made of cardiac patients at Englewood Hospital over a five-year period produced several interesting facts. For instance, men in the higher income groups seem to succumb to coronary disease at an *earlier* age than men of less wealth. The following table shows how male cardiac patients in two age groups were distributed among four income classes; Gordon [5] points out that in the suburban community from which most of the patients came, younger men who have reached the mid-middle or upper-middle income levels have done so "through fierce, hard climbing." Born into fairly low-income families, they have had to struggle hard to reach their present success. "In climbing so far so fast, they have exposed themselves to a great variety of stresses," he adds.

TABLE 6. *Distribution of cardiac patients according to income.*[5]

INCOME GROUP	PATIENTS UNDER 50 (% TOTAL)	PATIENTS 50-65 (% TOTAL)
Upper middle	24%	10%
	67%	44%
Mid-middle	43%	34%
Lower middle	26%	42%
	33%	56%
Lower	7%	14%

On the other hand, ironically enough, cardiac patients apparently stand a better chance of surviving their coronary attack if they are in the upper income levels, according to this study. The principal reason may be that, more economically secure, they can afford to stay in the hospital without the added strain of financial worries and are in a better position to heed the physician's advice to "slow down and stop working so hard."

The Emotional Price May Be Even Higher

The ambitious male—under both internal and external pressure to succeed and thus made to suffer feelings of guilt at real or apparent failures—pays an emotional price as well as a physical one. Although emotional problems do not bring a disproportionate num-

ber of men to psychiatric hospitals, they do express themselves in
"tension" symptoms, psychosomatic illnesses, vague physical complaints, and neurotic reactions. Two indicators of the heavier strain
under which men labor are obvious: both suicide and alcoholism
rates are substantially higher for men than for women. The suicide
rate for men, for instance, is generally three to four times that for
women, with the highest rate among men over 65—"the retired, the
unemployed and (in their own eyes) the unwanted." [1]

Even more so than in women, emotional problems in men tend to
be expressed as sexual dysfunction. "Psychological attitudes in the
male determine his sexual capacities more than any other factor,"
Swartz [6] states. "When he is under anxiety from any cause, his virility
will be threatened. A man can worry himself into impotence."
Swartz adds: "What nature deals out to man is kindness compared
to what he does to himself."

Resisting the Inroads of Time

Sexual problems in men tend to increase during middle age. Because of their more aggressive natures, men generally find it even
more difficult than women to accept the fact that aging brings an
inevitable decline in physical and sexual powers. Particularly if a
man's self-esteem is bound up in sexual performance, any decline in
ability can seriously threaten his sense of virility. Some men, therefore, become victims of a kind of "middle-age denial," which can
take many forms—affairs with younger women, divorces and remar-
riages, and a refusal to permit children to grow up.[1]

Some middle-aged men, too, go through what has been termed
the "male climacteric." They suffer from symptoms remarkably akin
to those of menopausal women: nervousness, depression, impaired
memory, inability to concentrate, easy fatigability, insomnia and loss
of sexual vigor. However, physicians frequently question the possibility of an actual male climacteric. "Ordinary clinical experience
arouses considerable skepticism," Swartz [6] writes. He points out that
the "sexual power in the male may be weakened by advancing years
but to no greater extent than any other bodily functions," and suggests that the symptoms of the "male climacteric" are usually the
result of psychoneurosis.

Masculinity—Inherent or Acquired?

All that has been written here suggests that men in general think,
feel and behave quite differently from women. Most would agree

that this is so. But what really accounts for the clear-cut distinction between the sexes?

Cultural training has a good deal to do with it. The imprinting of a gender role and gender identity—which begins at about 18 months and usually becomes "fixed" during the 3- to 6-year period—— depends to a large extent on environment: theoretically, boys and girls can choose either men or women to pattern themselves after. "What happens in the ordinary course of affairs," Money [7] explains, "is that pressures and rewards, both subtle and obvious, steer the boy infant to be imprinted to a male, usually the father, and a girl to a female, the mother, as the model from whom to pattern his or her own gender specific behavior."

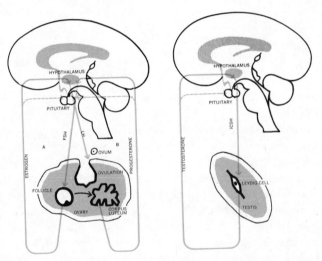

Fig. 25. Interplay of sex hormones differs in the female (left) and the male (right) mammal. In the cyclic female system the pituitary initially releases a follicle-stimulating hormone (FSH) that makes the ovary produce estrogen (colored arrows at A); the estrogen then acts on the hypothalamus of the brain to inhibit the further release of FSH by the pituitary and to stimulate the release of a luteinizing hormone (LH) instead. This hormone both triggers ovulation and makes the ovary produce a second hormone, progesterone (colored arrows at B). On reaching the hypothalamus, the latter hormone inhibits further pituitary release of LH, thereby completing the cycle. In the noncyclic male system, the pituitary continually releases an interstitial cell-stimulating hormone (ICSH) that makes the testes produce testosterone; ICSH acts on the hypothalamus to stimulate further release of ICSH by the pituitary. Broken arrows represent the earlier theory that the sex hormones from ovaries and testes stimulated the pituitary directly. (Levine, S.: Sci Amer 214:84, 1966.[10])

Most boys and girls then proceed to develop measurably different interests in life. In one of the most comprehensive studies of masculinity and femininity, Terman and Miles [8] state:

> From whatever angle we have examined them the males included in the standardization groups evinced a distinctive interest in exploit and adventure, in outdoor and physically strenuous occupations, in machinery and tools, in science, physical phenomena, and inventions; and, from rather occasional evidence, in business and commerce. On the other hand, the females of our groups have evinced a distinctive interest in domestic affairs and in aesthetic objects and occupations; they have distinctively preferred more sedentary and indoor occupations, and occupations more directly ministrative, particularly to the young, the helpless, the distressed.

A good proportion of "masculine" and "feminine" behavior, however, has clearly been learned, and a review [9] of subsequent sex and personality studies indicates that, as times and customs change, masculine and feminine interests have a way of changing as well.

The basic cause of the difference in sexual behavior patterns is presumably hormonal. (Physiologists are currently investigating one particularly intriguing theory: that all mammalian behavior patterns are basically female, and that male patterns are induced by the action of the sex hormone testosterone on the brain of the newborn animal.[10]) As Money [7] suggests, in men there may be an androgen-mediated phylogenetic vestige of the mechanisms seen in other mammalian species for the claim and defense of territory and breeding-ground rights. He points out:

> This conjecture helps take account of the greater geographical roaming of pubertal and adolescent males than females, their greater involvement in exploits of daring, adventure, and belligerence, their greater involvement in delinquency thereby, and their greater readiness to get into fights over their mates.

Clearly, whether the explanation lies in androgen levels or cultural training, the masculine man—with his aggressive, hard-driving and fiercely competitive nature—will be with us for some time to come. Which, on the whole, and despite its attendant problems, is probably all for the best.

CHAPTER 12 BIBLIOGRAPHY

1. Orr, D. W.: *in* Deutsch, A., and Fishman, H., eds.: The Encyclopedia of Mental Health, vol 1, New York, The Encyclopedia of Mental Health, A Division of Franklin Watts, Inc., 1963, pp. 126 ff.
2. Mead, M.: Male and Female, New York, Morrow, 1949, pp. 306-307.

    3. Knupfer, G., Clark, W., and Room, R.: Amer J Psychiat *122*:841, 1966.
    4. Gurin, G., Veroff, J., and Feld, S.: Americans View Their Mental Health, New York, Basic, 1960, pp. 233-235.
    5. Gordon, R. E., Gordon, K. K., and Gunther, M.: The Split-Level Trap, New York, Geis, 1961, pp. 86-88.
    6. Swartz, D.: Panel discussion, Canad Med Ass J *94*:207, 1966.
    7. Money, J.: *in* Deutsch, A., and Fishman, H., eds.: *op. cit.*, vol 5, pp. 1685-1686, 1705-1706.
    8. Terman, L. M., and Miles, C. C.: Sex and Personality, New York, McGraw-Hill, 1936, p. 447.
    9. Bieliauskas, V. J.: J Psychol *60*:255, 1965.
    10. Levine, S.: Sci Amer *214*:84, 1966.

ANXIETY AND THE FEMALE PSYCHE

M ODERN MEDICINE has removed from woman many causes for fears and anxieties to which she has been heir through the ages—notably fears about childbearing, high infant mortality and the generalized infections to which she was so vulnerable in the past. Yet modern society is now so constituted that other, perhaps more devastating, anxiety-producing situations have arisen—and in turn exact their psychological and physiologic toll.[1] Woman's motherly role and her historic role in homemaking have been greatly reduced by our culture. Her childbearing and child-care contributions to society diminished as the birth rate fell. Her usefulness as teacher and supervisor of her older children suffered as schools assumed more and more of the educational burden and as teaching the arts of homemaking and child care declined. And even today, if she seeks outside occupation, not only does she go into an environment where she frequently meets bias, but success in the work outside the home may bring about an even greater denial of her biologic female role.[2]

"With a sway no less whimsical than potent"

Every physician no doubt encounters, almost daily, examples of the emotional element that accompanies even the normal changes in a woman's reproductive physiology. "There is," states Dr. Doris Menzer, "the general emotional upheaval of the menarche, the premenstrual depressions and tensions, the frustration caused by dyspareunia and frigidity, the unhappiness of some who are not pregnant and others who complain that they are, and the instability of the menopause."[4] These are common experiences. However, in gynecologic diseases, more puzzling problems are frequently encountered. In 1843, Dewees, commenting on the "melancholies of menstrua-

tion," wrote that "it has been handed down to us from time imme-
morial, that the uterus exerts a paramount power over every other
system; and governs them [women] with a sway no less whimsical
than potent. That it creates, exalts or modifies diseases, in every
portion of the body." [5] But it is only recently that more objective
evidence has been marshalled concerning this interaction of physio-

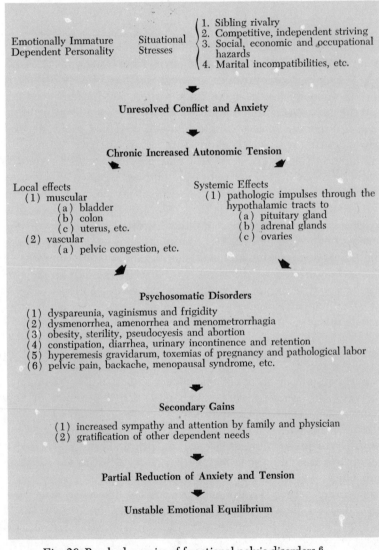

Fig. 26. Psychodynamics of functional pelvic disorders.[6]

logic and psychological factors in the disorders peculiar to woman (see Fig. 26) and, particularly, concerning the menses, which throughout the childbearing years are an ever-recurring symbol of her feminine role.

Menstruation—Badge of Femininity

Premenstrual tension, it has been said, is a condition known to many women but perhaps even better known to their husbands and children—victims of monthly personality change.[7] As with all menstrual disturbances, the pathogenesis is complex as physiologic and psychological factors meet. In a nutshell, while hormonal imbalance is responsible for fluid changes in tissue and for reactions of the autonomic nervous system, these, in turn, interact with psychic factors rooted in the personality development.[8] In its most severe form, premenstrual tension may be characterized by panic states, suicidal tendencies and psychotic delusional episodes.[9] And there is a growing awareness of its involvement as a factor in crimes of passion and violence.[10]

Again, in *dysmenorrhea*, it does not seem at all sufficient to classify the disorder as simply organic or functional: even when it is primarily organic, it has, usually, a functional overlay.[11] Investigations indicate that women who suffer from dysmenorrhea have a low pain threshold [8, 12]; this hypersensitivity increases their anxious anticipation and stimulates the emotional defenses against menstruation. Whereas the normal woman may have discomfort so trivial that she can almost ignore it, the psychoneurotic can build this into an agonizing pain [13] that may render her sick, helpless, or even rebellious against her fate.[8] As to the *amenorrheic* patient who begins to bleed at the first interview in the doctor's office, either following a pelvic examination or the withdrawal of a sample of blood for a laboratory test,[12] a diagnosis of emotional amenorrhea is at least a strong possibility. In less obvious cases, the tentative diagnosis of "hypothalamic" amenorrhea may follow when systemic and organic disease is ruled out in routine laboratory tests.[14] And even if a definite organic cause can be detected, most cases of amenorrhea will still be accompanied by "an insecurity, a conviction of reproductive incompetence and loss of femininity." [14] The desperate effort of a woman of 48 to "run away" [15] from a much feared hysterectomy, for instance, is pictured in the patient's "Draw-a-person" test (Fig. 27). But the controversy whether psychic or somatic influences are of greater importance in giving rise to distress is perhaps most marked in regard to the *menopause*.[1,16] Since the ovarian changes are very real, the question may resolve itself into that of

Fig. 27. Draw-a-person test executed on admission for hysterectomy by a 48-year-old woman (from Sturgis-Murawski [15]).

which occurs first—the somatic or the psychological factors (including the predisposition of a neurotic personality). This problem is still controversial,[1] although there can be little doubt that the menopause does represent deep psychological trauma, for the badge of femininity—menstruation—is now irretrievably lost.

Femininity Rejected—the "Atalanta Syndrome"

To some observers, the more refined and profound our understanding becomes, the more the dichotomy "somatic or psychic" seems to vanish altogether.[17] Such a guiding principle would call *first* for an understanding of the individual woman herself, particularly the way she accepts her feminine role, before approaching the management of her particular dysfunction. In this approach, wholehearted rejection of the "female role" is considered the prime focus of many somatic disorders. Given its name by O'Neill from the virgin huntress Atalanta (op. title p.), the syndrome is described as combining such various elements as *dyspareunia, frigidity, miscarriage, pregnancy vomiting* beyond the first trimester, *difficult labor,* and *failure of lactation*.[18] Women with a high "Atalanta count"—and with it a more complete rejection of femininity—also seem more prone to menstrual difficulties (pain being often less in prominence than malaise, distress, emotional upset and general disharmony in the sphere of sex adjustment).[18] Numerous studies discuss the higher incidence of these disorders in women who repudiate their roles as wives and mothers, reporting, for instance:

increased pregnancy vomiting in the presence of an ambivalent attitude of the mother toward the child [19, 20]

significantly longer active labor in women who viewed pregnancy as an illness [21]

more miscarriages and need for sedation during labor than in women who liked caring for their babies [2]

infertility as a result of psychogenic spasm of the fallopian tubes,[22] or of protective frigidity, vaginismus and dyspareunia (mechanically militating against proper timing or penetration).[23]

Admittedly, more extensive research is needed before the precise role of emotional insecurity in this type of patient becomes fully established. One basic question, for instance, seems to remain unanswered: granted the profound influence of the emotions on menstruation, why is there in some instances "a metrorrhagia, and in others amenorrhea, and at other times dysmenorrhea?" [12]

Like Mother Like Daughter

In a discussion of the role of emotions in the female patient, one more aspect, the mother-daughter relationship, merits consideration. Generally, the influence of the mother is a fundamental force in shaping her daughter's "feminine" development, both during the formative years and beyond. The little girl's innate femaleness directs her first emotional growth in step-by-step identification with her mother. This mother-daughter relationship comes fully to the fore at the *menarche*.[11] Whether the girl is given full biologic knowledge or not, emotionally her preparation by her mother for this event is most important, because it "includes the mother's unexpressed attitude toward her own menstruation. Thus the mother may communicate indirectly that something very painful is about to happen to the girl" [11] and thereby unduly increase the child's apprehensions. Or, if the first period occurs before the mother has seen fit to give enlightenment, the child may be filled with panic little relieved by belated explanations. Thus, at an early age, she may become "conditioned" by her mother, for life, to expect severe pain with her menses and to experience it, in due course, ever after.[24]

And when through the years an oversolicitous mother imbues her daughter with her own apprehensions regarding childbearing, such disturbed mothering capacity may well become self-perpetuating. In the end, such a problem-mother will produce a problem-daughter, who in turn may produce another of her kind.[25]

CHAPTER 13 BIBLIOGRAPHY

1. Kroger, W. S., and Freed, S. C.: Psychosomatic Gynecology, Glencoe (Ill), Free Press, 1956, pp. 44 ff., 370 ff.
2. Newton, N.: Maternal Emotions, New York, Hoeber, 1955, pp. 59 ff., 95 ff.
3. Campbell, E. M.: *in* Rogers, D. M., ed.: Depression and Antidepressant Drugs. Conf conducted at Metropolitan State Hospital, Waltham (Mass), Apr 20, 1960, pp. 55 ff.
4. Menzer, D.: New Eng J Med *249*:519, 1953.
5. Henriksen, E.: Clin Obstet Gynec *5*:252, 1962.
6. Mandy, A. J., et al.: Amer J Obstet Gynec *60*:605, 1950.
7. Weiss, E., and English, O. S.: Psychosomatic Medicine, ed 3, Philadelphia, Saunders, 1957, p. 374.
8. Benedek, T. F.: *in* Arieti, S., ed.: American Handbook of Psychiatry, vol 1, New York, Basic, 1959, pp. 727 ff.
9. Menzer-Benaron, D., *et al.:* in Sturgis, S. H., ed.: The Gynecologic Patient, New York, Grune, 1962, pp. 89 ff.
10. Paulson, M. J.: Amer J Obstet Gynec *81*:733, 1961.
11. Meares, A.: The Management of the Anxious Patient, Philadelphia, Saunders, 1963, pp. 65, 461.
12. Fluhmann, C. W.: The Management of Menstrual Disorders, Philadelphia, Saunders, 1957, pp. 223, 292.
13. Williamson, P.: Office Diagnosis, Philadelphia, Saunders, 1960, p. 378.
14. Menzer-Benaron, D., Sabbath, J., and Sturgis, S. H.: *in* Sturgis, S. H., ed., *op. cit.,* pp. 23 ff.
15. Sturgis, S. H., and Murawski, B.: in *ibid.*, p. 17.
16. Caldwell, W. G.: Med Times *88*:1007, 1960.
17. Deutsch, H.: Progr Gynec *2*:207, 1951.
18. O'Neill, D.: Practitioner *184*:749, 1960.
19. Chertok, L., Mondzain, M. L., and Bonnaud, M.: Psychosom Med *25*:13, 1963.
20. Ringrose, C. A. D.: Canad Med Ass J *84*:1064, 1961.
21. Rosengren, W. R.: J Nerv Ment Dis *132*:515, 1961.
22. Greenhill, J. P.: Office Gynecology, ed 7, Chicago, Yr Bk Pub, 1959, p. 166.
23. Morris, T. A., Taymor, M. L., and Sturgis, S. H.: *in* Sturgis, S. H., ed.: *op. cit.,* pp. 199 ff.
24. Sablosky, L.: Med Times *90*:555, 1962.
25. O'Neill, D.: J Obstet Gynaec Brit Comm *66*:762, 1959.

THE PANICKY PATIENT

THE ANXIETY-PANIC REACTION is an acute, subjectively dramatic incident: in it, the anxiety literally overwhelms the patient who may feel as though he is "disintegrating."[1] Typically, the attack comes on suddenly and without warning, the extreme apprehension being expressed through widespread autonomic discharge. Often, a sense of impending doom is manifested in such expressions as "I am dying," "This is the end," "Oh my God, I am going."[2] The tapering-off period can be prolonged. Sometimes, the prepanic level is never quite regained; and after his first attack the patient may live in constant fear and dread of another one.[1] How does this flood of emotional, sensory and motor excitement come about? By what mechanism does it deprive the patient of all his self-control?

Low-level vs. High-level Anxiety

While any degree of anxiety brings on a characteristic lowering of intellectual control and concentration, at *low* levels of anxiety there is at the same time a general alerting of the organism. In this state of preparedness (see Chapter 1, "Fight or Flight"), the patient may even develop improved performance and an increased ability to cope with danger.[3] Not so at *higher* levels of anxiety: as stress and anxiety mount inordinately, apprehension increases to terror; overalertness reaches the stage where the patient makes violent and unpredictable responses to even minor stimuli.[4] Consequently, there is a tendency to rigidity of response and a decrease in the patient's ability to act effectively. The very organization of behavior breaks down, regression to simpler and more primitive modes of response occurs, and all aspects of psychological functioning are affected.[3]

Clinically, this is manifest in the great distractibility, generalized irritability, and random-appearing behavior of the panicky patient. In the words of Basowitz *et al.*, "It is as if the central control mechanisms were disordered."[3] Indeed, the acute state of panic can be so dramatic, so out of control and overwhelming as to suggest added participation of the midbrain, along with its cortical origin.[1]

Psychiatric Emergencies—Human Emergencies

In addition to *intensity* of anxiety as a determining factor of panicky response, other factors are obviously involved. One of considerable importance concerns the specific nature of the threat—which may be as complicated as a homosexual panic or as commonplace as a child's nightmare. But in spite of the fact that the various types of acute anxiety states can look strikingly different, and that some may seem extraordinarily difficult to comprehend, they have much in common. Psychiatric emergencies are human emergencies, after all. And they are more or less stereotyped since threats to human existence are somewhat limited in variety and tend to produce rather simple, elemental types of response in all people. Whatever the type of psychiatric emergency, however, the task of the physician who meets it is, first, to analyze the situation and, second, to minimize the threatened harm.[5]

NATURAL HISTORY OF A PANIC REACTION

Psychologically, acute anxiety attacks are often set off by stimuli that are essentially symbolic—circumstances that owe their force not to their intrinsic quality but to their meaning to the patient.[6] The attack usually begins with a distressing fear or sense of imminent dissolution or loss of mind.[7] This fear need not, however, have a topical content, and the individual may even lack awareness of the emotional basis of his attack. Employing what is psychiatrically termed "secondary defense," he often denies most vehemently the presence of a difficulty in precisely the area where it exists.[1] Within a few seconds or minutes, the distressing physiologic concomitants of anxiety follow (see Figs. 28, 29, 30). Related to gross over-

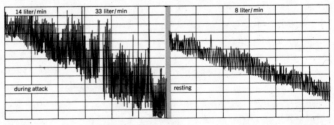

Fig. 28. Increased respiratory rate during acute anxiety attack. Oxygen consumption rose in the patient from 8 liter/min during the resting state to 33 liter/min during the attack.[7]

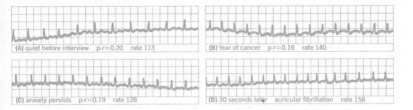

(A) quiet before interview   p-r=0.20   rate 113
(B) fear of cancer   p-r=0.16   rate 140
(C) anxiety persists   p-r=0.19   rate 128
(D) 30 seconds later   auricular fibrillation   rate 158

Fig. 29. Depression of the S-T segment followed by atrial fibrillation during stressful interview precipitating acute anxiety.[6]

activity of the sympathetic nervous system, they embrace tachycardia, hypertension, hyperactive deep reflexes, trembling, sweating, giddiness and many other objective signs. Hyperventilation may dominate the picture with resultant paresthesias of the legs, fingers and hand, or even carpopedal spasm.[7, 8] Polyuria occurs frequently.[6] And somatic complaints may be diffuse or sometimes focused on one organ such as the heart, the lungs, or the gastrointestinal tract.[8] Attacks tend to take place in crowds, subways, tunnels, churches and movies; but often they awake the patient from a sound sleep.[7]

A Difficult Differential Diagnosis

In spite of—or perhaps because of—this wealth of signs, the task of accurately diagnosing an acute anxiety attack is not always easy. Patients whose basic problem is one of anxiety, for instance, are not infrequently referred to cardiac clinics—hardly surprising in view of the frequent prominence of palpitation, skipped beats, troubled

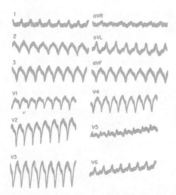

Fig. 30. Ventricular tachycardia attack accompanying emotional conflict with anxiety in patient with no other evidence of heart disease.[6]

breathing and chest pressure.[1] And Garmany feels that a good many urgent referrals to the psychiatrist with a diagnosis of "acute anxiety state" are in fact suffering from depression.[9] The diagnostic difficulties arise from a number of factors. For one, the physician is much more likely to hear a descriptive after-the-fact account than he is to be an on-the-spot witness [1]; even when he does witness an attack, these true emergencies usually leave little time for deliberate and cautious evaluation.[5] Second, a wide variety of primary somatic conditions may in turn be accompanied by anxiety attacks—for instance, Graves's disease and various types of cardiovascular and pulmonary disturbances. These primary somatic disorders, none genuinely threatening to life, may present the symptoms that also accompany primary panic reactions. Finally, panic states must be distinguished from other psychiatric conditions, particularly early schizophrenia and agitated depression. Incipient schizophrenia always should be suspected in the young introvert who presents anxiety symptoms for which no clear psychogenesis is apparent. On the other hand, in the middle-aged patient exhibiting symptoms of apprehension and agitation, agitated depression is a distinct possibility.[4]

The differential diagnosis of pure anxiety states therefore demands both the recognition of the signs of anxiety and the exclusion of other physical or psychological disorders. Or, when there are signs of anxiety together with a physical or other psychological disorder, the relative importance of each must be assessed.[4] In recognizing the attack for what it is, a list of the more common somatic, neurologic and psychiatric conditions that must be considered in the differential diagnosis of the acute anxiety state may be of importance: see Table 3. No combination of signs and symptoms will consistently establish the diagnosis of an anxiety attack, of course. But once organic disease has been ruled out, the differential diagnosis can often proceed at a less hurried pace. Usually, the final diagnosis can be made by a shrewd assessment of the circumstances, surrounding an attack in the light of some knowledge of the personality, goals, attitudes and vulnerabilities of the patient—information adduced through painstaking history of the patient and contact with members of his family and his friends.[6]

"Emotional Death"—Reality?

While often terrifying to observe, the acute anxiety attack is essentially a benign, transitory phenomenon.[6] By allowing the patient to

TABLE 7. *Conditions to be considered in the differential diagnosis of anxiety neurosis* [7]

MEDICAL	GYNECOLOGIC AND OBSTETRIC
1. Thyroid disease	1. Menopausal syndrome
2. Heart disease	2. "Pseudoparoxysmal nocturnal dyspnea"
(a) Coronary disease	NEUROLOGIC
(b) Paroxysmal atrial	1. Diencephalic autonomic epilepsy
tachycardia	2. Epilepsy
(c) Cardiac asthma	3. Brain disease
3. Asthma	PSYCHIATRIC
4. Anemia	1. Early schizophrenia
5. Addison's disease	2. Endogenous depression
6. Hyperinsulinism	3. Other neuroses

talk about himself, and by being calm and reassuring in both word and action, the physician can nearly always quiet the patient's agitation or distress.[5] Psychopharmaceutic medication may be indicated, particularly in anxiety warranted by reality,[10] or if there is marked insomnia.[4] Nevertheless, in occasional instances, attacks may be prolonged and the patient may reach a point of physical collapse.

As to "emotional death," this has long been a subject of considerable controversy.[1] In studies concerned with this topic, Richter [11] points to bradycardia—rather than tachycardia—as a possible factor resulting from vagal stimuli under stress. Such vagal effects were experimentally produced by Richter, and survival rate was greatly shortened in the animals as, under the setup of the experiment, their "terror and hopelessness" were stepped up. Emotional "voodoo death," proposed Cannon, "may be real" and "it may be explained as due to shocking emotional stress—to obvious or repressed terror." Certainly, he adds, "if it is authentic it deserves careful consideration." [12]

CHAPTER 14 BIBLIOGRAPHY

1. Laughlin, H. P.: The Neuroses in Clinical Practice, Philadelphia, Saunders, 1959, pp. 38 ff.

2. Adams, R. D., and Hope, J. M.: in Harrison, T. R., et al., eds.: Principles of Internal Medicine, ed 4, vol 1, New York, McGraw-Hill, 1962, p. 391.

3. Basowitz, H., et al.: Anxiety and Stress, New York, McGraw-Hill, 1955, pp. 12 ff.

4. Meares, A.: The Management of the Anxious Patient, Philadelphia, Saunders, 1963, pp. 337 ff.

5. Gwartney, R. H., et al.: JAMA 170:1022, 1959.

6. Wolf, S.:The acute anxiety state, DM (Disease-a-Month), Oct. 1960.

7. Hope, J. M.: GP 24:(9), 135, 1961.

8. Remmen, E., et al.: Psychochemotheraphy, Los Angeles, Western, 1962, pp. 17 ff.

9. Garmany, G.: Brit Med J 2:115, 1955

10. Modell, W.: Relief of Symptoms, ed 2, St. Louis, Mosby, 1961, p. 132.

11. Richter, C. P.: Psychosom Med 19:191, 1957.

12. Cannon, W. B.: ibid., p. 182.

THE HYPOCHONDRIAC

T HE PATIENT who seems to make a career of being unduly preoccupied with the state of his own health is familiar to most physicians, too familiar, some might wearily suggest. He was also well known to the early Greeks, who assumed that his endless and mysterious ills resulted from a disorder of the hypochondrium, the upper lateral region of the abdomen below the lowest rib, and that the spleen in particular was the seat of the disorder.[1]

But through the ages physicians have suspected that more than physical factors were involved in the hypochondriac's "illnesses." Roughly a century ago, Forbes Winslow gave a surprisingly modern description of the syndrome: *"That psycho-somatic disease termed hypochondriasis, which manifests itself principally in a morbid anxiety as to the health, is in its primitive nature, essentially a diseased concentration of the attention upon, and consequent exaggeration of conditions of physical sensibility, resulting often from slight bodily ailments which eventually assume to the distempered and deluded imagination a grave and significant character."* [2]

While an exaggerated concern over physical health is the distinguishing characteristic of all hypochondriacal conditions, there obviously are varying degrees of "morbid anxiety" involved: the stout middle-aged lady who worries about her "elimination problems" is hardly in the same class as the gentleman who complains that his insides are rotting away. James suggests that hypochondriacal phenomena might be arbitrarily divided, though with some overlapping, into 3 categories: 1. the personality trait of body overconcern; 2. hypochrondriacal anxiety; 3. hypochrondriacal delusions.[3]

The Patient "Overaware" of the Body Processes

A certain amount of concern over the state of one's health is common, even praiseworthy. We expect intelligent individuals to follow rules of good hygiene, keep their weight within certain limits, watch for "danger signals," have regular physical examinations. Too, in almost every person's lifetime, some degree of overconcern is occasionally to be expected, particularly during periods of stress such as puberty, early marital adjustment, the menarche and the approach of old age—and, of course, in time of illness.

The "mild" hypochondriac, however, appears chronically overconcerned with his health, or at least some aspect of it. He is a perpetual worrier. Because his attention is focused on subjective bodily sensations, he often becomes alarmed by those normally below the threshold of awareness, such as the "pounding in the head" which is simply his own pulse beat magnified by the pressure of a pillow. And, since he is keenly aware of the minor aches and pains that go unnoticed or at least unremarked by less sensitive subjects, he not only complains more—he has more to complain about. The French sometimes call hypochondria *la maladie du petit papier* because of the written list of symptoms the patient frequently carries with him.

For many such individuals, lifelong overconcern about health is so ingrained and habitual that it might well be considered a personality trait. Frequently, the mild hypochondriac is found to have been raised in an atmosphere of illness by persons who made much of illness or physical complaints. Throughout life, whatever insecurity he feels is unconsciously translated into concern over physical well-being. Nevertheless, despite his constant complaints and numerous aches, the "never well" person does not appear too handicapped by his health worries. In many instances, he manages to carry on a busy, even successful, life.

The Highly Anxious Hypochondriac

The hypochondriac who suffers persistent social disability or much personal distress because of his chronic "ill health" cannot be dismissed as lightly, of course. The aches and pains this patient brings to the physician are often severe enough to cause genuine invalidism. Moreover, this patient may be operation-prone. In women, gynecologic operations are the commonest, and Kemp [4] notes that they often are in a progressive scale of D&C repair, amputation of cervix, oophorectomy, hysterectomy, bladder neck surgery, and so on. He suggests that surgeons do their best to recognize such a patient early and deny her "another plank in the platform of her disability programme."

In this more emotionally troubled patient, hypochondriasis is clearly a neurotic symptom. The patient's excessive anxiety is, in effect, displaced from its unconscious mental sources to one or more body organs, which then become the center of affective distress and preoccupation.[5] The organ unconsciously chosen is usually one particularly subject to physiologic expressions of anxiety, such as the GI tract. But almost any part of the body can be affected, and some individuals simply experience a vague, general discomfort. They may complain of chronic feelings of weakness and fatigue, perhaps, along with insomnia, irritability and "shifting" aches and pains.

As might be expected, the hypochondriac derives various benefits from his quite real suffering.[1, 6] He gains primarily, as suggested above, from the fact that preoccupation with somatic matters serves to keep conscious attention away from unpleasant and anxiety-arousing feelings—from aggressive, hostile or sexual wishes. On an unconscious level, there are also important self-punitive elements subserved by the "giving" of a serious illness to oneself. Many individuals have an unconscious conviction of guilt because of real or imagined misdeeds. The hypochondriac can at least partly assuage this guilt through his suffering. And there are a number of secondary gains to be derived from a serious illness, even an imagined one.

A serious illness, for instance, serves as an escape from many painful and intolerable life situations. It can be used as an excuse for personal and business failures, as a reason for avoiding unwanted responsibilities or postponing difficult decisions, as a means of evoking love and attention from others. Then, too, many hypochondriacs seem to get a feeling of physical identity from their illness, as though the fact that the head aches, proves, if nothing else, that it *exists*. And finally, it has been suggested that many hypochondriacs nurse themselves to compensate for the loving attention they failed to receive as children.

For these and other reasons, the hypochondriac often appears reluctant to surrender his symptoms and is not impressed to hear that nothing is organically wrong. As Kemp[4] wryly notes, "One is left with the conclusion that examinations and investigations reassure only the doctor."

Prelude to Psychosis

Hypochondriacal symptoms are also fairly common in many psychotic syndromes, particularly in schizophrenia, involutional melancholia and certain other depressive reactions.[1] Thus, a particular patient's gradual withdrawal of interest in the external world and his increasing somatic and physiologic self-absorption may be the early signs of serious emotional disorder.

In most instances, the physician soon recognizes those symptoms bizarre enough to imply a break with reality. In early schizophrenia, for instance, hypochondriacal delusions often reflect the chaotic sexuality of the process: there may be pregnancy fantasies, delusions of sex changes, ruminations about masturbation, sexual performance, change in physical features. And in depressive psychoses, delusions tend to have a nihilistic quality: the patient believes his bowels are blocked up, his intestines have rotted away, his head is completely empty.[3]

Occasionally, however, the dividing line between a neurotic and a psychotic symptom may be blurred indeed. Psychiatric consultation may be indicated whenever the patient's degree of hypochondriacal preoccupation is severe, prolonged, handicapping, associated with other neurotic symptoms, or appears to be increasing.

Management of the Hypochondriac

Treatment of the hypochondriac can be a frustrating experience. He may seem to be getting a certain satisfaction out of being sick, and—as discussed above—he usually *is*. Yet the hypochondriac is not a malingerer: both his suffering and his symptoms are quite real, and often he will respond to the warm and sympathetic physician. To help facilitate therapy, it has been suggested that the physician: [6]

1. *Listen to the patient.* Allow him to express feelings with his mouth rather than with his body. Encourage him to put into words his frightening and unacceptable thoughts and fears.

2. *Avoid overstudying him.* Hypochondriacs are not immune to serious disease, of course, and an adequate examination is always essential. But a long and unnecessarily detailed workup alarms this already anxious individual. It also strengthens his conviction that there really is something wrong—the doctor just can't find it.

3. *Give simple anatomic and physiologic explanations for each symptom.* The patient may be reassured to see that emotions can cause, for instance, a distinct and observable spasm, which in turn can cause real and painful symptoms. Because the hypochondriac has a vivid imagination, however, it is important to be sure that he understands each term used. Graphic material and much repetition are often helpful.

4. *Help him see the "use" of his illness.* In some patients, after encouraging them to discuss their various life problems and difficulties, it may be possible to help them see how they are "using" their illnesses. This is

not always possible, but the appropriate patient, indirectly or directly, can be shown how, by centering his attention on his health, he is trying to avoid looking at or dealing with other problems in his life.

To sum up: because hypochondriacal anxiety stems from psychological conflict, the patient's somatic complaint will seldom respond to reassurance alone, except temporarily. "Therapy," James advises,[3] "should aim at understanding the conflict situation, dealing with the anxiety and helping the patient to find a more satisfactory solution to his life situation."

CHAPTER 15 BIBLIOGRAPHY

1. Laughlin, H. P.: The Neuroses in Clinical Practice, Philadelphia, Saunders, 1956.
2. Winslow, F.: Obscure Diseases of the Brain and Mind, ed 3, London, Robert Hardwicke, 1863, p. 265.
3. James, I. P.: Med J Aust 2:521, 1960.
4. Kemp, R.: Lancet 1:1223, 1963.
5. Noyes, A. P.: Modern Clinical Psychiatry, ed 4, Philadelphia, Saunders, 1953.
6. Wahl, C. W.: Psychosomatics 4:9, 1963.

Fright, HONORÉ DAUMIER. Pencil (?) and charcoal
Courtesy of THE ART INSTITUTE OF CHICAGO: *Gift of* ROBERT ALLERTON

ANXIETY AND GUILT

T HE PROBLEM of guilt is inextricably interwoven with the problem of anxiety." [1] This intimate link informs whatever approach is chosen in probing guilt problems—whether by defining what constitutes guilt, or by studying initial guilt stirrings in the child, or by considering the relation of guilt to more composite emotions involving also shame, hate or depression. And it is this close tie of guilt to anxiety that makes guilt feelings so important in personality development and the treatment of emotional disturbances.

What Is Guilt?

Guilt has been defined as a form of anxiety and depression by Schottstaedt.[2] In the description of others, it appears as a sense of unworthiness, a painful emotion, arising in a person who has violated the prohibitions of his conscience.[3, 4] It involves a need for punishment in combination with a fear of punishment.[5] The violation that arouses the feelings of guilt may have occurred not only in reality but also in fantasy: characteristically, patients with psychiatric disorders may assume guilt, and often express guilty feelings, when there is no legitimate reason.[6] Indeed, guilt feelings, since they result from transgression against the moral or ethical standards one has set for oneself, are especially internal and personal.[3] They are also often composite feelings, including, at different times, anxiety (due to fear of punishment), depression, longing (out of fear of loss of love), and shame (which makes a guilty individual wish to hide).[7]

How does a "Sense of Guilt" Develop?

There is no evidence to indicate that infants experience a sense of guilt: rather, they are anxious about parental retributions. Children past the age of six, on the other hand, apparently do experience guilt in much the same fashion as adults.[8] What has happened between these two stages to account for the change?

In the view of many, the capacity for guilt feelings originates with

111

the child's realization that he has an independent personality and that, in exploring its potential, he inevitably acts against the people he loves and depends on.[3, 9] In the process of overcoming this dilemma, the child develops his "conscience," or "superego" if you will, which henceforth is to be his very own set of values concerning right or wrong, good or bad. Guilt feelings now arise as the behavior profile sanctioned by the conscience is violated.[7, 10] This genesis explains some of the motives that bring a guilt-ridden patient to the physician: he may simply consider the physician as a new authority who, in lieu of his parents, now has the right to stand in judgment of his unacceptable thoughts or behavior.[4] And, in some difficult patients, hostility feelings toward the physician or analyst may repeat the patient's negativistic and stubborn "me-do-it" phase of early childhood.[9]

How Guilt and Anxiety Interact

Guilt has been referred to as "moral anxiety."[5] And with this term, the close kinship of the two emotions, guilt and anxiety, finds both appropriate and succinct expression. The mastery of guilt feelings may become the all-consuming task of a person's whole life, just as the mastery of anxiety may.[11] Even at their earliest stage, when guilt feelings first form in the child, they are accompanied by anxieties that center on the parent, whose retaliation is anticipated and feared.[10] Later, with the establishment of a fully developed conscience, the anxieties and guilt feelings focus on the individual's own self; the fear of external punishment is now superseded by dangers threatening from his "frustrated" conscience.[5, 11] Inversely, in some patients, anxieties may not be the cause but the effect of guilt feelings; such a patient, as he represses guilt-provoking incidents or attitudes, may exhibit disturbing anxieties for which he himself often cannot account.[3]

Even in the area of somatization reactions, the genetic relation to anxiety is evident: a bad conscience may produce the same intestinal, circulatory and respiratory sensations as anxiety. "My heart is heavy," or "I am not able to breathe freely" may be expressions of troubled conscience.[11] Again, when "shame" is experienced, the feelings of guilt appear intermingled with those of anxiety—an anxiety of anticipated or actual discovery.[5] In approaching his patient's guilt complexes, therefore, the physician's primary effort can be directed

toward locating and controlling the anxieties and frustrations behind
the self-punitive feelings.

The Guilt-Ridden Person and His Neuroses

As pathogenic guilt utilizes all the neurotic evasions, in order to
maintain the status quo without assuming real responsibility for
one's behavior, it becomes actively involved in many neurotic and
somatic disorders, as shown in some of the examples below.

Quite obviously, neurotic compulsive rituals—such as compulsive
handwashing, for instance—often represent symbolic attempts to
achieve moral purity or to relieve guilty feelings.[12, 13] Guilt also has
an important role in the psychodynamics of the alcoholic which
Knight traces as thwarted self-indulgence, hostility, guilt feelings,
the need for punishment and, ultimately, alcohol.[14] Overcompen-
sated guilt feelings are also said to account for the frequent arro-
gance of alcoholics.[15]

In war neuroses, guilt feelings were found to be a factor particularly in instances of the loss of a comrade toward whom the patient
entertained ambivalent feelings.[12, 13] Open psychotic breakdowns
may be triggered, in "borderline" cases, by guilt feelings that follow
indulgence in sexual or other pleasures.[16] Still another guilt-distor-
tion of personality is manifest in the patient who feels less guilty if
someone else can be made to feel guilty. Such a mechanism is based
on the familiar observation that "feelings of guilt which give rise to
anxiety may be alleviated if one is able to cast the blame for shameful tendencies or wishes onto the outer world." [13] In the course of
the process, such patients may attach to a person whom they make
feel guilty if he or she refuses to do what the patient wants.

Somatic Manifestations of Guilt

Guilt feelings may also give rise to or prolong somatic illness;
most of the somatization reactions known to be connected with anxiety and depression can follow guilt states, emphasizing again the
closeness of the three emotional conditions.[2] Dynamics that can link
guilt, anxiety and depression are shown in Figure 31.[17]

Outwardly, the guilt-ridden patient often betrays his guilt feelings
by less erect carriage and a less resilient step; subjectively, he may
suffer generalized discomfort akin to that in anxiety.[8] When he is
sick, the importance of the disease often appears to him out of pro-

portion—not infrequently from a sense of guilt related to early sex activities or indiscretions.[13] Typically, guilt feelings are connected with intestinal sensations; and reduced gastric function and colitis have been observed as somatization reactions: bronchial asthma, rosacea, hysterical whispering are other examples of the manifold somatic dysfunctions that have been directly or indirectly linked to exaggerated guilt feelings.[8, 11, 18-20] Feelings of guilt have also been invoked as instigators of stammering. Without knowing why, explains Rado, the stammerer "gets scared. Guilty fear promptly stops his speech as if to warn, 'Watch your words.'"[21] This mechanism explains why the stammerer's speech is undisturbed when he is alone, sings or recites in a group—all instances where he dispenses with his anxieties.

Are Guilt Feelings Treatable?

In assisting the guilt-ridden patient in his plight, the physician will find many therapeutic avenues open to him. Principally, he can approach guilt through its close relationship to anxiety. When tranquilizers or other suitable calming psychotropics are employed, the patient often becomes more willing to express his guilt feelings as

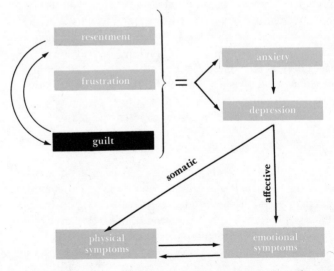

Fig. 31. Simplified chain of emotional interaction—with guilt, anxiety and depression as important links (*Schematized and adapted from* S. F. Moore, Jr.[17]).

his anxieties abate. He may then explore his personality problems more readily, be better able to profit from counseling, and, generally, to face reality. A patient type most likely to profit from medicinal tranquilization is, for instance, the overanxious, insecure, excessively inhibited individual whose upbringing has been overly dutiful and strict, and who, as a result, has developed anxieties and guilt feelings that interfere with the normal functioning of his personality.

Another form is frequently seen, "guilt in young mothers." "I can't think what I've done, Doctor. He's had the same food as usual, and all his vitamins and everything, and now he's come out in this rash. What can I have done?" This, or something like it, has probably been heard often enough by the family doctor, particularly from a primipara. While their genesis may be controversial, such guilt feelings are undesirable, since they "may lead to overanxiety, which in turn gives rise to psychosomatic complaints." [22] And the physician may take medical steps to control such intensive feelings of anxiety and remorse.

In addition to pharmacotherapy, patient rapport can serve as a means in helping the patient to a better control over his feelings of guilt and anxiety. Certainly, the physician is invested with many of the qualities the patient once recognized in his own parents at the time his conscience was forming; and this fact alone should allow him to adopt an advantageous attitude of firm authority and of a limit-setting disciplinary force.[4]

"Suppose," says Dr. Levitsky in his illuminating study of the role of guilt in emotional problems, the patient ". . . considers himself unworthy, perhaps, because he does not do enough for his family. He makes it clear that this is despicable on his part. He implies that in some way or other he should undergo pain and punishment. . . . In a great many situations I have found it very useful to ask the patient how he would behave if a friend were to come to him with a similar problem. Would he display the same punitive, rejecting attitude towards the friend, and call him despicable and not fit to live with?" [23] Most of the time, the patient replies that, on the contrary, he would tend to be sympathetic and supportive. Merely pointing out this simple difference is an eye opener to many patients, and a huge relief. Undoubtedly, guilt feelings also tend to inhibit the normally aggressive and competitive spirit of the individual.[3,5] Here, encouragement of more critical attitudes towards elders, or toward cultural patterns in general, is worthwhile for patients whose self-esteem otherwise would be in jeopardy.[23]

In summing up ways that he found helpful with patients suffering from "excessive conscience" and presenting themselves as sinful and guilty, Dr. Levitsky primarily advises that "to locate the anxiety and frustration behind the self-punitive feeling" is the best means of therapeutic approach to the guilt complex.[23]

CHAPTER 16 BIBLIOGRAPHY

1. Stern, K.: The Third Revolution, New York, Harcourt, 1954, p. 184.
2. Schottstaedt, W. W.: Psychophysiologic Approach in Medical Practice, Chicago, Yr Bk Pub, 1960, p. 129.
3. Jenkins, R. I.: in Reymert, M. L., ed.: Feelings and Emotions, ed 1, New York, McGraw-Hill, 1950, pp. 353 ff.
4. Daniels, P. S.: Postgrad Med 32:436, 1962.
5. Sappenfield, R. G.: Personality Dynamics, New York, Knopf, 1954, pp. 182 ff., 401.
6. Salzman, L.: Compr Psychiat 2:179, 1962.
7. Ostow, M.: in Arieti, S., ed.: American Handbook of Psychiatry, vol 1, New York, Basic, 1959, pp. 73 ff.
8. Hofling, C. K.: Textbook of Psychiatry for Medical Practice, Philadelphia, Lippincott, 1963, p. 68.
9. Munroe, R. L.: in Arieti, S., ed.: op. cit., vol 2, pp. 1461 ff.
10. Ewalt, J. R., Strecker, E. A., and Ebaugh, F. G.: Practical Clinical Psychiatry, New York, McGraw-Hill, 1957, pp. 29 ff.
11. Fenichel, O.: The Psychoanalytic Theory of Neurosis, New York, Norton, 1945, pp. 105 ff., 136, 138, 183, 496 ff.
12. Laughlin, H. P.: The Neuroses in Clinical Practice, Philadelphia, Saunders, 1956, pp. 393, 614, 668 ff.
13. Noyes, A. P., and Kolb, L. C.: Modern Clinical Psychiatry, ed 6, Philadelphia, Saunders, 1963, pp. 49, 415, 443, 451.
14. Zwerling, I., and Rosenbaum, M.: in Arieti, S., ed.: op. cit., vol 1, pp. 626 ff.
15. Gal, P.: J Amer Geriat Soc 12:1128, 1964.
16. Schmideberg, M.: in Arieti, S., ed.: op. cit., vol 1, p. 414.
17. Moore, S. F., Jr.: GP 31:100, 1965.
18. Dunbar, F.: Synopsis of Psychosomatic Diagnosis and Treatment, St. Louis, Mosby, 1948, pp. 104 ff., 120 ff.
19. Wittkower, E. D., and White, K. L.: in Arieti, S., ed.: op. cit., vol 1, p. 697.
20. Alvarez, W. C.: The Neuroses, Philadelphia, Saunders, 1951, p. 322.
21. Rado, S.: in Arieti, S., ed.: op. cit., vol 1, pp. 336 ff.
22. Rayner, C.: Med World (London) 94:533, 1961.
23. Levitsky, A.: Amer J Clin Hypn 5:127, 1962.

ANXIETY AS A REACTION TO FAMILY ILLNESS

TO SAY that patients have families is like saying that the diseased organ is a part of the individual. Both facts seem too obvious to discuss, yet for a long time neither received due recognition from the medical profession." But, just as the concept of an isolated diseased organ was replaced by the recognition of the totality of the sick person as the unit of practice, so, in a further step, the patient is now increasingly considered not simply by himself but as a member of the family unit or constellation.[1] "The environment in which an individual lives is much more than a physical world; it consists of the close interpersonal interaction within the family group" and of the socio-economic structure in which the individual and his family live.[2] "In many respects," says Rosen, "the family relationship resembles what physicians call a 'closed energy system,'"[3] "A change in one part of the family, e.g., the absence or illness of a member, cannot fail to have tremendous reactions *throughout* the family insofar as established homeostatic modes of adjustment and behavior sequences are altered and various members' security threatened."[4]

Psychodynamics of Family Life

In the view of Nathan W. Ackerman, emotional disturbance in the individual should be approached through analysis of the psychological content of his family experience. A "conveyor belt for anxiety and conflict,"[6] the family can "make or break the emotional health of its members."[7]

Among the most upsetting events in family relationships is the severe illness of a member—whether mental, emotional, or somatic. While at times the family faces the fact of illness realistically, "frequently family members react inappropriately in terms of their fears and resentment," making the illness much more troublesome for the patient. Unable to control or conceal their own anxiety, the family may aggravate the patient's, and they may emphasize the un-

favorable outcome of comparable illnesses in friends or acquaint-
ances to intensify the patient's fears further. Apparently, this is their
way of handling their own anxiety in the presence of illness.[8]

The anxiety-provoking potential of illness has been increased by
social and cultural changes in the familial relation to the sick role.
"Formerly, the petition to be ill was legitimized largely within the
family, and the individual strain of illness was met, with or without
formal medical help, by a temporary or even permanent reorganiza-
tion within the family to support an effective sick role for one or
more of the members." [9] Today, modern medical care, as well as that
of hospitals, has largely superseded the family in this function and
thereby deprived the family of the gratification that went with its
helping role.

The emotional reaction in the family to the illness of one member
is conditioned by several factors:

The role the ill member has played in the family ("It makes
considerable difference whether a child, the mother, the father, or
some elderly person in the family is ill," [10]) the reaction (and the
age level) of the person who is emotionally affected by illness of a
family member toward health and illness in general, toward the
specific illness in particular, toward his own goals in terms of work
and independence, and his feelings about how his future might be
affected by the outcome of the illness, and the nature of the primary
illness.

The following discussion reviews the anxiety reactions in the family in general to some primary illnesses, and analyzes these disruptive effects in terms of the individual family members who are
the emotional targets of the illness.

The Family of the Psychiatric Patient

"A great deal of thought has been devoted to the mentally ill
member, but relatively little consideration has been given to the rest
of the family who must live with him." [11] Yet "mental illness and its
treatment influence not only the patient but the groups of which he
is a member. In the case of the family, these effects may be far-
reaching and of great magnitude." [12] Mental illness of one member
usually shows itself in abnormal life patterns, deviant behavior and
disturbed interpersonal difficulties. This, in turn, is reflected in
strained family relationships. "The result may be anxiety for all
members of the household and guilt and feelings of rejection for
some." [13]

After reviewing 105 records of families with a mentally ill member, M. B. Treudley finds that generalizing about the types of effects such illness has on the family is difficult because of the variation in contributions each member makes to the whole family. When mental illness overtakes a parent, the effects on the children vary with their age and sex. They may have to stay away from school to substitute for the mother in performing her home duties; or they may have to watch her so that she will not get into trouble. The feelings of extreme anxiety, guilt, shame, and inferiority that mental illness often arouses may follow the child to school. The social stigma attached to mental illness may bar the child from the neighborhood play groups or submit him to unmerciful teasing and tormenting. It is not always the younger children who suffer most, however. Adolescents, also, may be greatly burdened—especially adolescent daughters, who feel isolated and deprived of their home as a status-defining agency.[11]

As for mates, when one partner becomes mentally ill, at first the other partner attempts to see the deviant behavior within the framework of normality; this involves considerable effort and struggle.[12] Gradually, with the growing perception of the ill mate's actual condition, final, painful recognition of true illness develops and is acknowledged.[14] In the opinion of Treudley, the indirect effects of a wife's mental illness, for instance, in undermining her husband's self-confidence and in sapping his energy, have not yet been fully appreciated.[11] A severely depressed member, whose suicidal threats call for incessant anxious surveillance by all those living with him, can jeopardize the entire family's tranquillity.

There are "shameful" as well as "respectable" sick roles in our society; severe psychiatric illness belongs to the former.[9] M. B. Treudley, while sifting over 100 records of families that harbored a mentally ill member, found serious social stigma as well as "feelings of extreme anxiety, of guilt, of shame and inferiority"[11]—feelings that follow a child of such a family to school. Among examples of ostracism occurring with the cruelty characteristic of youth, she cites two: the bitter memories of a girl made an outcast from neighborhood groups by the quarrels her mentally ill mother started; and the emotional experiences of a boy who had to run after a police wagon in order to pick up clothing his mother was discarding from the van that was taking her to a mental hospital.[11]

Impact of Alcoholism

The onset of alcoholism often precipitates cumulative crises in the alcoholic's home. "The unpredictability of the situation, added to its lack of structure, engenders anxiety in family members which gives rise to personality difficulties."[15] Many wives of alcoholics exhibit serious neurotic tendencies. Where the wife is the alcoholic, the family often attempts to hide her from the condemning eyes of society. While some alcoholics may manage to keep their marriages alive, others head increasingly for complete separation from the family or for divorce. Of all members in the family of the alcoholic, the children are probably the most adversely affected: in the battles between the alcoholic and the nonalcoholic parent, the child becomes "a frequent source of conflict and an innocent and malleable instrument."[16] A number of these children eventually become alcoholics or drug addicts themselves, or later exhibit psychiatric disturbances traceable to their early environment and relationships within the family.[6]

The Slowly Grinding Borderline Neuroses

In addition to major neuroses or psychoses, even minor emotional deviations of a family member can have undesirable repercussions within the family. For instance, a domineering mother or mother-in-law "can be the cause of anxiety, hostility and neurotic symptoms in either wife or husband."[17] Or an impotent husband may arouse feelings of hostility and anxiety in his wife—hostility because she is sexually frustrated, anxiety because she thinks she may be at fault.[18] The impact of the family on the child's potential for healthy or pathological development has been acknowledged by Freud.[12] Many disturbed parent-child relationships may be traced back to the parents' personality structure, their emotional problems, bias, and past childhood experiences.[2]

Parental dissensions, hostility, cruelty, neglect, overprotection or excessive ambition for the child—all can be responsible, in great part, for neurotic reactions and personality difficulties in the youngster. Preoccupation with the child's intellectual abilities—a likely outgrowth of maternal self-doubt—may make the mother punitive toward the child if he does not perform to meet her expectations. Or the mother may pressure the child to fulfill some special maternal fantasy. If the child is unable to rise to such unrealistic, external demands, mental illness may result.[19] A common source of later personality difficulties is the broken home. The unwed mother, often herself the product of a home lacking in affection, may have difficulty in giving adequate affection.[20] Even conflicts that have existed between the parents and *their* parents can affect a couple's ability to relate to their child.[2] These patterns of psychologic "contagion," as Ehrenwald terms them, produce a slow, grinding friction of emotional and mental interactions between persons. And, based on observations, he suggests that these attitudes may be cumulative in effect over several generations, increasing along the line and abrasive in their contagious potential.[5]

A Handicapped Child

The frequency of parental anxieties about the physical integrity of their unborn and the normality of their newborn anticipates, in some measure, the desperate feelings with which parents view biological handicap in a child.[2] "It is probably accurate to state that emotional disorganization occurs in every family having a chronically ill or handicapped child, particularly during the early period of adaptation." "In the process of discovering and recognizing the handicap, most parents show great fear, anger, guilt, confusion, bewilderment, and the seeking for medical magic. There is usually an exacerbation of the parent's preexisting neurotic tendencies and an increase in marital discord and misunderstanding." [21] Blindness or deafness in an infant, for instance, can be so overwhelming a discovery to parents that they need psychological help.

Treatment of neurologic conditions—epilepsy, for instance [23]—as well as of neurotic disorders, requires work with the parents to relieve their anxiety and gain their cooperation.[24] Such family therapy is designed to avoid secondary emotional problems in the child and his family, including the siblings, who, under the physician's advice and guidance, should be assured of an equal share of the parents' time and attention.[25] Discussion of the parents' anxieties with a physician frequently reduces their intensity and alleviates the parents' sense of isolation.[21] Parental reactions, of course, vary with the individuals and with the type of defect in the child. If the defect is one that is not obvious physically, parents may initially attempt to deny its reality. This sets up a wall between the mother and the father, who pretend to each other that there is no real handicap.[26] Afraid to surrender this pretense, it becomes increasingly harder for them to talk to each other about the family's real problems, and their emotional relationship is likely to grow distant.

A Mentally Subnormal Child

On discovering that they have a mentally subnormal child, parents usually experience profound shock. They may suffer groundless personal guilt, or partially, perhaps, blame their marital partner.[27] The mother, in particular, often sees the misfortune as a retribution for an earlier sexual indiscretion.[28] She frequently is the one to realize, much earlier than the father, that something is quite wrong with her child—especially if she has older, normal children.[29] Sooner or later, the parents must face the heartrending decision whether such a child should be institutionalized. In making the decision, their emotional stability, particularly that of the mother, counts heavily.[30] And, of course, the emotional impact on the normal siblings must be given careful evaluation.[31] A handicapped child, even when accepted affectionately by his brothers and sisters, is disturbing to them to some degree. They may hesitate to bring other children home to play because they fear the remarks their friends make ("Your brother's dumb. He can't walk or talk or anything" [26]). For sisters in the family, the retarded sibling may become a "dating embarrassment." [32]

Effects of Serious Somatic Illness

In the following, diabetes, cardiac disease and tuberculosis are discussed because they exemplify, though by no means exhaust, classes of serious somatic illnesses, which, when they affect one family member, have a typical potential for causing anxieties in other members of the family.

DIABETES

It has been said "that when a child develops diabetes the doctor immediately has two patients—the child and the mother." [33] Even this must be considered an understatement because, as Dolger and Seeman point out: "Not only are the child and the mother affected, but so are the father, the other children, in-laws and relatives, friends and sometimes even teachers." The possibility of hereditary factors may burden the parents with unconscious guilt feelings.[33] Furthermore, the daily routines of urine tests, medication and special eating schedules can be a harassing chore to the mother. "Relatives, especially grandparents, can be very harmful to a child's morale if their reactions are tinged with overanxiety and hysteria." And the siblings, depending on their own degree of security and adjustment, may resent the special attention the diabetic child must receive.[33]

HEART PATIENT

With the heart recognized by the laity as vital to life, it is not surprising that a high degree of familial apprehension should center on a family member's *cardiac condition*. Among the family reactions elicited in an interview with the mothers of 25 children with congenital heart disease were: "vague apprehension about the behavior of the newborn, uncertainty about the diagnosis, anxiety about the child's symptoms. . . ." [34] Several mothers "recalled with feeling the anxiety they suffered because of chronic fear of losing their child." Emphasized among the anxiety-producing situations were the parents' decision about surgery, their shocked reaction to the child's postoperative appearance, and "their anxious wait for the degree of success of the surgical procedure." At an outpatient clinic for children, it was considered anxiety-relevant that in suspected heart disease the father accompanied the child and mother on the first visit in 50% of cases (as compared to 17% in noncardiac conditions).[35] "The doctor says she's got a bad heart . . . but it's us who suffer, not her," commented one of the mothers of the 100 children randomly selected for this study. Adult cardiac patients often give rise to similar anxiety reactions within their families: the problems and needs of 250 family members of adult cardiovascular patients—wives, husbands, daughters, sons or other close relatives investigated in a pilot study—revealed anxiety and tension levels often so high as to immobilize the entire family; and to prevent, during a critical situation, even the hearing of medical explanations.[36]

TUBERCULOSIS

Among infectious diseases, active tuberculosis has been cited as an example of an illness that may contribute to disease in other family members—not necessarily by dissemination of the infection but by psychic disruption of the family unit. The mobilization of feelings of guilt or shame toward the sick person, the increased burden on the mate—all these are psychological stresses that may initiate an anxiety reaction, a phobia, or a behavioral disorder.[37]

The Terminal Patient

The chronic nature and constant pain of terminal carcinoma may place excessive stress upon the family's emotional ties with the patient.[38] When a family member tends to deny the reality of a patient's cancer, it is because "the anxiety is too great for him to cope with all at once." [39] Sometimes the physician is made the target of an irrational hostility from the family, "as if the tragic facts were of his making. In such situations," states Marmor, "it behooves the doctor to remain objective and understanding, since at such a time the emotionally upset family members become his patients too, so to speak." Occasionally it may seem preferable to keep the diagnosis of malignancy a secret from the patient, but to share it with a family member.[38] This can produce many difficulties. A daughter, for instance, who has been told secretly that her mother suffers from cancer, herself suffers great anxiety and inadvertently communicates that fear and concern.

With the psychologic insight of the artist, Aldous Huxley in *Point Counter Point* describes the emotional relationship of John Bidlake, the grandfather ill with cancer of the stomach, to little Phil, the grandson stricken by meningitis. The grandfather's anxieties of having to die soon are inordinately enhanced by his grandson's desperate condition. Every unfavorable bulletin from the nursery makes him shudder. The family learns to understand and respect his weakness, scrupulously avoiding allusions to what is happening upstairs. In Huxley's own words: John Bidlake "had always hated the spectacle of suffering and disease, of anything that might remind him of the pain and death he so agonizingly dreaded for himself. And in this case he had a special reason for terror. For with that talent for inventing private superstitions which had always distinguished him, he had secretly decided that his own fate was bound up with the child's. If the child recovered, so would he. If not. . . ." And at the precise time of the youngster's death—as if sensing it—the old man takes to bed with an attack of pyloric obstruction.

Yet another artistic account of a tragic family ordeal is John Gunther's *Death Be Not Proud—a Memoir*. While telling of the gallant fight of his own son, who died at 17 of a brain tumor, the father-author inadvertently bespeaks the harrowing tensions and incessant anxieties that beset the parents, from the first diagnosis until the fatal end.

Helping the Family to Help the Anxious Patient

There are instances, principally in the care of children, where the psychotherapeutic effort may be directed mainly toward the figure upon whom the patient is primarily dependent,[40] instead of the patient himself. "We can't help Johnny learn to read until we help Mother," commented a speaker at a panel discussion chaired by Dr. J. E. Slutsky at a meeting on "Theory and Treatment of Emotional Disorders in Children," sponsored by the Council of Psychoanalytic Psychotherapists, Inc.[41] Other participants concurred, stating that

"Successful treatment of emotionally disturbed youngsters must also include investigation and, often, treatment of the entire family." Sometimes the most apparently disturbed member of a family "may actually not be the cause of the real trouble; he may be a scapegoat, 'acting out' the feelings of parents or others."

In certain situations, helping an anxious family may also help the somatically ill patient who causes the anxiety. Examples are cardiac conditions in which control of anxiety and tension in the surrounding family may assist the patient in his adjustment and recovery [36]; or cases of diabetes, where allaying of parents' fears, as well as correcting the psychological attitude of all involved, can be most important factors in the patient's proper adjustment.[23, 33, 42] In critical or terminal illness when the patient is a child, the relief of parental feelings of guilt and anxiety may enable the parents to divide their time more effectively between the ill child and the healthy siblings.[21] The physician may further protect the siblings by counseling the parents on how to handle their reactions to the death of the child. At times, for instance, a young sibling may act out the circumstances of death in play. This may be helpful for the resolution of the child's anxiety, but—unless they are properly prepared— is often difficult for bereaved adults to tolerate.

Patient History is Family History

Because so important a part of the patient's psychic life is tied to that of his family, any approach to his emotional problems warrants a thorough sifting of the family history. It is here that the roots of the presenting difficulties of the anxious patient can frequently be found. During this inquiry, particular alertness to epochs of family life during which anxiety was prevalent can be fruitful. Next, the interview may turn to "Who lives with you now?" and thereby move from the patient in the office to the absent family members, who "are nevertheless a shadowy presence." [43] The answers should un- cover areas of tension that may ordinarily go unnoticed—many of them based on neurotic behavior patterns, psychosomatic conditions or somatic illnesses of members of the patient's family. The tradi- tional term "family practitioner" actually implies such an approach.[1] And whether, in the end, interviews are conducted with the anxious patient and his family at the same time (as it usually was by the old- time family doctor) or separately may depend on the circumstances of the individual case. In family interviewing, it is often possible to make the "family ghosts" emerge more quickly. "Frequently, what one parent conceals, the other reveals; what the parents together hide, the children ferret out"; and, generally, what one member distorts, another corrects.[43] With the insight obtained, the targets for psychotherapy can be more judiciously chosen—whether the tense and anxious patient at hand, a disturbed or ill family member, or both.

CHAPTER 17 BIBLIOGRAPHY

1. Richardson, H. B.: Patients Have Families, New York, Commonwealth Fund, 1948, pp. vii, xv, xviii.
2. Noyes, A. P., and Kolb, L. C.: Modern Clinical Psychiatry, ed 6, Philadelphia, Saunders, 1963, pp. 97, 484 ff.
3. Rosen, V. H.: in Eisenstein, V. W., ed.: Neurotic Interaction in Marriage, New York, Basic, 1956, p. 208.
4. Albert R. S.: Arch Gen Psychiat (Chicago) 3:682, 1960.
5. Ehrenwald, J.: Neurosis in the Family and Patterns of Psychosocial Defense, New York, Hoeber Med Division, Harper, 1963, pp. ix, 128 ff.
6. Ackerman, N. W.: The Psychodynamics of Family Life, New York, Basic, 1958, pp. vii ff.
7. ——: in Deutsch, A., and Fishman, H., eds.: The Encyclopedia of Mental Health, vol 2, New York, The Encyclopedia of Mental Health, A Division of Franklin Watts, Inc., 1963, p. 613.
8. Holland, B. C., and Ward, R. S.: in Arieti, S., ed.: American Handbook of Psychiatry, vol 3, New York, Basic, 1966, p. 359.
9. Stainbrook, E.: in Arieti, S., ed.: ibid., vol 1, p. 152.
10. Schottstaedt, W. W.: Psychophysiologic Approach in Medical Practice, Chicago, Yr Bk Pub, 1960, pp. 172-173.
11. Treudley, M. B.: Ment Hyg 30:235, 1946.
12. Spiegel, J. P., and Bell, N. W.: in Arieti, S., ed.: op. cit., vol 1, 1959, pp. 116, 131, 133 ff.
13. Clausen, J. A., and Yarrow, M. R.: J Soc Issues 11:(4)3, 1955.
14. Yarrow, M. R., et al.: J Soc Issues 11:(4)12, 1955.
15. Jackson, J. K.: Quart J Stud Alcohol 15:562, 1954.
16. Gelber, I.: Alcoholism in New York City, NY Dept of Health, City of NY, Ryder Press, 1960, pp. 12, 17 ff.
17. Weiss, E., and English, O. S.: Psychosomatic Medicine, ed 3, Philadelphia, Saunders, 1957, p. 117.
18. Orr, D. W.: in Deutsch, A., and Fishman, H., eds.: op. cit., vol 3, p. 844.
19. Shainess, N.: in Arieti, S., ed.: op. cit., vol 3, p. 62.
20. Stevenson, G. S.: Mental Health Planning for Social Action, New York, Blakiston, McGraw, 1956, pp. 216 ff.
21. Garrard, S. D., and Richmond, J. B.: in Lief, H. I., Lief, V. F., and Lief, N. R., eds.: The Psychological Basis of Medical Practice, New York, Ryder Press, 1963, pp. 370, 377, 380 ff., 391, 398.
22. Davidman, H.: in Lief, H. I., Lief, V. F., and Lief, N. R., eds.: ibid., pp. 405 ff.
23. Gallagher, J. R.: Medical Care of the Adolescent, ed 2, New York, Appleton, 1966, pp. 222 ff., 376 ff.
24. Settlage, C. F.: in Nelson, W. E., ed.: Textbook of Pediatrics, ed 8, Philadelphia, Saunders, 1964, p. 92.

25. Bartram, J. B.: *in* Nelson, W. E., ed.: *ibid.*, pp. 1246 ff., 1251 ff.

26. Spock, B., and Lerrigo, M. O.: Caring for Your Disabled Child, New York, Collier, 1965, pp. 12 ff., 37 ff.

27. Ewalt, J. R., Strecker, E. A., and Ebaugh, F. G.: Practical Clinical Psychiatry, ed 8, New York, Blakiston, McGraw-Hill, 1957, pp. 169 ff.

28. Aldrich, C. K.: Psychiatry for the Family Physician, New York, Blakiston, McGraw-Hill, 1955, p. 115.

29. Getz, S. B., and Rees, E. L.: The Mentally Ill Child, Springfield (Ill), Thomas, 1957, p. 40.

30. Yannet, H.: *in* Nelson, W. E., ed.: *op. cit.*, pp. 1241 ff.

31. Boggs, E. M., and Jervis, G. A.: *in* Arieti, S., ed.: *op. cit.*, p. 33.

32. Stern, F. M.: *in* Deutsch, A., and Fishman, H., eds.: *op. cit.*, vol 4, p. 1199.

33. Dolger, H., and Seeman, B.: How to Live with Diabetes, New York, Norton, 1958, pp. 129 ff.

34. Glaser, H. H., Harrison, G. S., and Lynn, D. B.: Pediatrics *33*:367, 1964.

35. Apley, J., Barbour, R. F., and Westmacott, I.: Brit Med J *1*:103, 1967.

36. Vavra, C. E., Urbain, L. S., and Shaw, A.: Amer J Public Health *56*:1507, 1966.

37. Cohen, S.: Mind *1*:153, 1963.

38. Zarling, R.: *in* Schiffren, M. J., ed.: Management of Pain in Cancer, Chicago, Yr Bk Pub, 1956, pp. 211 ff.

39. Marmor, J.: *in* Lief, H. I., Lief, V. F., and Lief, N. R., eds.: *op. cit.*, pp. 313 ff.

40. Hofling, C. K., ed.: Textbook of Psychiatry for Medical Practice, Philadelphia, Lippincott, 1963, p. 513.

41. Fifth Annual Scientific Conference on Psychoanalysis, New York, February 26, 1967: Reviewed in Science News *91*:246, 1967.

42. Weinberg, A.: *in* Deutsch, A., and Fishman, H., eds.: *op. cit.*, vol 4, pp. 1368 ff.

43. Ackerman, N. W., and Richardson, H. B.: *in* Lief, H. I., Lief, V. F., and Lief, N. R., eds.: *op. cit.*, pp. 547 ff.

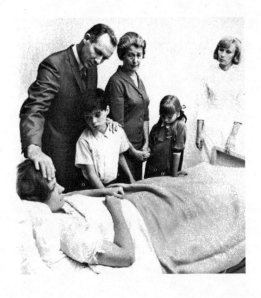

EARNING A LIVING IN TODAY'S ANXIOUS WORLD

A FTER HAVING LIVED alongside primitive Kanakas in Polynesia and Indians in the mountains of Mexico, and after having observed their lazy ways of life, their joyous loafing, their utter unconcern for time, and their habit of going to bed at sunset," reflects Professor Alvarez, "I marvel that we Americans, with much the same nervous system as the primitive person has, can drive at our work all day and late into the night. I doubt if the Great Designer ever intended the human brain to work so constantly or at such high pressure, and I marvel that so many persons can stand the grind as long as they do." [1] While Dr. Alvarez did not so state specifically, his implication, of course, is that for the many who can stand the high pressures, many others cannot.

Fig. 32. Two worlds.

Competitive Ambition: Thwarted Aggression: Gnawing Anxieties

Western man has a heritage of acquisitive and aggressive drives. Competitive ambitions form an integral part of his personality.

Work and financial success are essential measures of his competitive prestige. Thus, a man's job is not only a means of earning a living but also a way of establishing himself as an adult. Whatever threatens his competitive ambitions may produce profound anxiety.

The ways in which anxiety arises in this emotional drive for competitive prestige are many and subtle. They are listed by Dr. May [2] as emanating from:

1. isolation and alienation from others,
2. hostility produced by competitive individualism,
3. self-alienation as one views one's self as the object of the market, or makes one's feelings of self-strength dependent on a function of extrinsic wealth rather than intrinsic capability and productivity.

Moreover, the person who feels anxious about his lack of success tends to try even harder—thus setting up a vicious cycle (Fig. 33) that may increase his isolation, hostility and anxiety, unless therapy can succeed in breaking the trend.

Fig. 33. Mechanism operative in the contemporary long-run increase of "competitive anxiety." (Adapted from May, R.[2])

Emotional Illness by Professional Class

That "keeping up with the Joneses" often finds its repercussion in emotional illness has been repeatedly observed. Redlich and his collaborators [4] noted the higher incidence of neurosis in higher social levels. In similar observations, Seward [5] stressed particularly the significance of ambivalence and status strivings in the emotional conditions of middle-class people. Faris and Dunham [6] demonstrated that the rate of first admissions to a mental hospital from various areas of Chicago was highest around the central business district, lowest on the city's periphery. Based on the classic New Haven study, by Hollingshead and Redlich,[7] of patients under psychiatric care, Figure 34 gives some highly significant findings on the relationships between social class and mental illness. It shows the prevalence of neurotic (rather than psychotic) conditions among business, professional and managerial personnel, and the types of neuroses that affect these groups as well as those of employees, workers, and laborers.

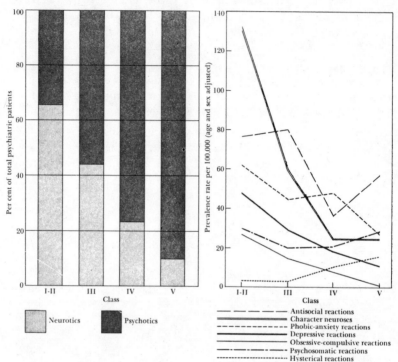

Fig. 34. Class status and (*left*) types of mental illness, neuroses cf. psychoses, (*right*) types of neuroses. Classes were established on the basis of position, education and residence: I. Business and professional leaders (3.4%); II. Managerial class (9%); III. Employees, technicians, semiprofessionals (21.4%); IV. Skilled manual workers, semiskilled, clerical and sales workers (48.5%); V. Semiskilled factory hands and unskilled laborers (17.7%). (Adapted from Hollingshead, A. B., and Redlich, F. C.[7])

In Pursuit of the "Perpetually Unattained"

A good deal of attention has been directed in recent years to the emotional and mental health of executives. One reason for this was the assumption that much can be learned about the nature of stress by closely observing people who constantly carry great responsibilities.[8] A canvass of corporation medical directors on emotional problems of executives emphasizes their innately high-powered personalities and aggressive energies, which produce abrasive relationships with others.[9] Because of their high-drive achievement desire, many successful business executives labor under a "sense of the perpetually unattained" and suffer the anxieties that accompany this incessant drive.[10]

New evidence that psychogenic ulcers may indeed be related to the stress of responsibility has been adduced in experiments performed by J. V. Brady of the Walter Reed Army Institute of Research in Washington, DC (see Fig. 35). In this setup, two mon-

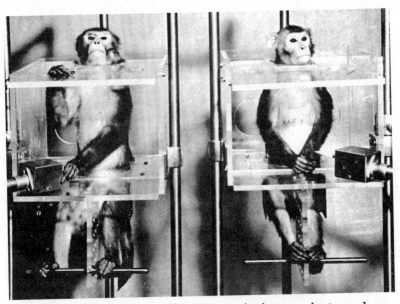

Fig. 35. Both animals receive brief electric shocks at regular intervals. The "executive" monkey (*left*) has learned to press the lever preventing shock to both animals. The control monkey (*right*) has lost interest in its lever, which is a dummy. Only "executive" monkeys developed ulcers. (Adapted from Brady, J. V.[11])

keys were subjected to a stressful situation by regularly applying electric shocks to their feet. One—the "executive" monkey, Brady called it—was supplied with a key, which, properly used, would prevent the shocks to both animals; the other—the "employee" monkey—had no such gadget. Result: Only the "executive" monkey developed ulcers; the "employee" monkey, who participated in the experiment in the same way as the other monkey but without "executive responsibility," showed every evidence of good health at the completion of the test. This experiment, performed many times with different pairs of monkeys, achieved the same general result.[11, 12]

Job Security: Two-edged Sword

While the emotional drain on a person at the assembly line or the drawing board may not match that on an executive, the average employee still has an ample share of competitive situations in which advancement, success, and failure are constant aspects of the job. Even today, job security continues as the single most important consideration. "The feeling of helplessness without job security produces anxiety and this, in turn, precipitates various symptoms." [13]

Unfortunately, security can be a two-edged sword—emotionally. "The anxious patient," says Meares, "who is only just able to keep going, needs all the help he can get in the way of social security. He needs security of employment, so that he is relieved of the anxiety that he may not be able to provide for his wife and family. . . . Yet, when the individual is robust, these same influences may tend to produce anxiety because of the routine, the lack of variety, and the very boredom that security brings." [14]

Another anxiety-precipitating factor is the "at-work situation." Working conditions, company policies or personal animosities can be an unending source of anxieties and tensions, which the alert physician may spot from signs and symptoms that his patient displays. Nor is it unusual for the physician to see patients who are plagued by fears simply because they have been given job responsibilities beyond those that they think they are capable of carrying.[13]

The Boss

One target of frustrated aggression at work—inveighed against more often, perhaps, than any other—is "the boss." It is common experience for the physician to hear a patient blow off steam about his superior when, in fact, he gives very little explanation for his acute hostility. This frustration at work often combines with domestic problems.[14] Recall the familiar story of the man, criticized by his boss, who in turn had an argument with his wife; she spanked the child, the child kicked the dog, and the dog chased the cat. Moreover, if the home situation involves uncontrolled children, or perhaps a wife who habitually takes the boss's side, the unfortunate man's aggression and anxiety are further complicated.

"I Don't Know Where I Stand"

While actual job loss is, of course, the more serious threat, many patients suffer anxieties because they feel that they are not making progress on the job. Such a patient, when questioned closely by the physician about his at-work situation, may blurt out, "The trouble is, I don't know where I stand." Furthermore, many people today live uncomfortably with the threatening realization that they can readily be replaced by machines.

These feelings of anxious insecurity often have their roots in the beginning experiences of the infant and child: being hired or fired has been likened, psychologically, to the early childhood experience of being given or denied love and affection.[13] Even early feeding methods can reinforce or undermine a man's later feelings of security about his livelihood.[15] And throughout adolescence, school examinations provoke anxieties that are the typical forerunners of later feelings of anxiety, which may alert or paralyze the adult who faces threats to earning his livelihood.

To Be One's Own Boss

Unwillingness to accept the authority of others (and the accompanying frustrations) may lead a person to seek work in which he is his own boss. This in turn imposes new and different aggressions, worries and fears.

Many a businessman takes his problems of indignation and anger against competitors home, battling with the unsolved at night or over weekends. The professional man, too, as Meares reminds us, "is threatened by the competition of his colleagues. Even the research worker in his ivory tower is not free from it. Somebody else may be on the verge of the same discovery." [14] And because civilized living does not allow these aggressions to find direct expansion, anxiety results.

Too Much Work or the Wrong Kind

Overwork, formally ascribed an important place in the etiology of emotional and mental disorders, is now held, at least in its abnormal forms, to be a symptom rather than a cause of emotional dysfunction. The compulsive neurotic may work excessively hard to diminish anxiety; the individual harassed by feelings of inferiority may derive ego support from overwork; or the withdrawn person may find hard work a means of reaching others on a neutral, nonthreatening plane.[16]

On the other hand, current thinking also holds that anxieties and tensions can develop from certain types of work. Strain and tension, for example, may arise from jobs that lack incentive or, on the contrary, are surrounded by turbulence and turmoil. Persons of creative ability are particularly prone to anxiety because the realities of life and of subsistence often conflict with the idealistic needs of their personalities. A frequent problem case seen by the physician is the writer or artist who complains that he cannot produce as he feels he should, or that he has failed to live up to the high hopes of his youth. Driven by today's economic pressures, all he did, perhaps, was to make money, whereas he wanted originally to be a writer or artist of stature.

"The Job Has Been My Life"

Paradoxical but commonly observed is the fact that, while during the active work years the *frustration* of aggression has been an endless source of stress and anxiety, the step of retirement, the *renouncing* of aggression, is often a new cause of anxiety. At retirement, no matter how much economic security a man has, he still must face the realization that he is no longer considered so capable as before and that a younger man is taking his place. "The job has been my life," many will say to express the feelings of rejection that they suffer at compulsory retirement. Analytically, retirement has been interpreted as a "reverse adolescence," in which the return is made from independence back to dependence—with a reawakening of whatever dependency problems have remained unsolved and repressed.[17] If a patient lacks the flexibility to meet this new challenge, he will develop anxiety and depressive reactions, which may present themselves to his physician in the guise of neurotic symptoms.

Changing the Patient's Work Outlook

When a patient presents an emotional problem clearly connected with earning a living, treatment is of course directed first at the emotional reaction proper. Pharmacotherapy may not only lessen anxiety but help make the patient more communicative and receptive to the physician's suggestions. Since it is usually almost impossible to change the conditions of employment, the physician may attempt to change the patient's outlook on life and attitudes to his work. The emotional disturbance at hand will offer ample opportunity for discussing the patient's relation toward employer and fellow employees, and also for assessing his ambitions, resources and talents.

If the patient seems incapable of achieving the goals he is pursuing, his physician may try, carefully and gently, to decrease the demands the patient makes on himself so that they become more realistic, more consistent with his capacities. The physician may also stress the need to "see the other fellow's side of the argument" and the wisdom of accepting, with grace, a certain amount of failure in life. The time-honored recommendation "to take a vacation," if practicable, or to develop some hobby or interest that may give some satisfaction or feeling of accomplishment outside the job, may help the patient see the need for leading a life better balanced in terms of work, goals, rest, exercise and play.

In large factories, the insights of industrial psychiatry are being utilized more and more. In the smaller world of his office, the physician can often help the patient who suffers from status anxieties or job tensions to regain emotional health.

CHAPTER 18 BIBLIOGRAPHY

1. Alvarez, W. C.: The Neuroses, Philadelphia, Saunders, 1955, pp. 136, 247 ff.
2. May, R.: The Meaning of Anxiety, New York, Ronald Press, 1950, pp. 181 ff.
3. ———: in Masserman, J. H., and Moreno, J. L., eds.: Progress in Psychotherapy, New York, Grune, 1957, p. 86.
4. Redlich, F. C., et al.: Amer J Psychiat 109:729, 1953.
5. Seward, G.: Psychotherapy and Culture Conflict, New York, Ronald Press, 1956, pp. 101 ff.
6. Faris, R. E. L., and Dunham, H. W.: Mental Disorders in Urban Areas, New York, Hafner, 1939.
7. Hollingshead, A. B., and Redlich, F. C.: Social Class and Mental Illness, New York, Wiley, 1958, pp. 223-234, 248.
8. Ewalt, J. R., and Farnsworth, D. L.: Textbook of Psychiatry, New York, Blakiston, McGraw-Hill, 1963, p. 337.
9. Terhune, W. B.: Industr Med Surg 32:167, 1963.
10. Newcomb, T. M.: Social Psychology, New York, Dryden Press, 1950, pp. 408 ff.
11. Brady, J. V., et al.: J Exp Anal Behav 1:69, 1958.
12. Wooldridge, D. E.: The Machinery of the Brain, New York, McGraw-Hill, 1963, p. 131.
13. Levinson, H.: in Deutsch, A., and Fishman, H., eds.: The Encyclopedia of Mental Health, vol 6, New York, The Encyclopedia of Mental Health, A Division of Franklin Watts, Inc., 1963, pp. 2027 ff.

14. Meares, A.: The Management of the Anxious Patient, Philadelphia, Saunders, 1963, pp. 84, 94, 295.
15. English, O. S., and Pearson, G. H.: Emotional Problems of Living, ed 3, New York, Norton, 1963, pp. 21 ff.
16. Noyes, A. P., and Kolb, L. C.: Modern Clinical Psychiatry, ed 6, Philadelphia, Saunders, 1963, p. 99.
17. Aldrich, C. K.: Psychiatry for the Family Physician, New York, Blakiston, McGraw-Hill, 1955, pp. 196 ff.

*I want my job to be important enough for a good
salary, not important enough to warrant automation.*

CAN ANXIETY BE MEASURED?

ALTHOUGH precise levels may not be obtainable with methods currently available, anxiety *can* be measured to some degree. A number of psychological tests are in existence today that, in skilled hands, not only reveal a great deal of information about the patient's emotional state but also give a fairly good idea of his "anxiety level."

"Screening out" the Anxious Patient

Among the most widely used psychological tests, for instance, are self-rating questionnaires—lists of printed questions to which subjects reply with a "yes" or "no." An important advantage of these tests is that they can be used with large groups of people (they were, in fact, first developed to screen out undesirable draftees during World War I). Generally speaking, they are not difficult to administer or score, and can be counted on to spot many, if not all, emotional disorders.

Of these "personality tests," the Minnesota Multiphasic Personality Inventory (MMPI) is the unquestioned leader. Developed at the University of Minnesota in 1941, it was "designed ultimately to provide in a single test, scores on all the more important phases of personality." [1] After the patient has answered its 550 questions, he usually has revealed much of his health concerns, his family and marital problems, his sexual attitudes, his religious, social and political points of view, and his phobias and delusions, if any. The MMPI also contains built-in scales that indicate how truthful the subject is being and how well he understands the questions.

More practical clinically, the patient's responses are compared with norms established for the test's various categories, which include hypochondriasis, depression, psychopathic deviations, paranoia and schizophrenia. Significant deviations from the norm in one or more of these categories may indicate mental imbalance.

THE ANXIETY SCALE

In addition to the 10 test categories, other scales have been derived from the MMPI. Taylor,[2] for instance, selected questions judged by many to be indicative of anxiety, and, after comprehensive testing, evolved the Taylor Manifest Anxiety Scale. Some of the 50 questions she and her co-workers considered most discriminatory between anxious and nonanxious individuals (with the "anxious" answers) include:

I am often sick to my stomach. (True)
I am about as nervous as other people. (False)
I blush as often as others. (False)
I have diarrhea ("the runs") once a month or more. (True)
When embarrassed, I often break out in a sweat, which is very annoying. (True)
Often my bowels don't move for several days at a time. (True)
At times I lose sleep over worry. (True)
I often dream about things I don't like to tell other people. (True)
My feelings are hurt easier than most people. (True)

This anxiety scale has been used in research and in clinics since its development.

ROLE OF THE COMPUTER

Because of its length and complexity, scoring the MMPI and assigning a clinical profile to a patient is a time-consuming procedure. In recent years, however, the task has been simplified through the use of electronic computers. At the Mayo Clinic, where the MMPI is routinely given to incoming patients, electronic computers have now scored over 20,000 of these tests. The clinic's computer is even equipped to give capsule descriptions of a patient based on his test. Thus, if the patient's depression score falls within normal limits, the machine prints: "Views life with average mixture of optimism and pessimism." If the paranoia scale falls within normal limits, the machine tells the physician: "Respects opinions of others without undue sensitivity."[3]

Computer diagnoses may be on the increase, but there are still a number of shorter and simpler psychological questionnaires that the clinician can use either to screen large groups of patients or to serve as an aid to diagnosis of an individual patient. An example is the Cornell Medical Index, which asks the patient to answer 195 informally worded questions "designed to correspond to the questions usually asked in a comprehensive medical history." The first section of the Index is concerned with the patient's somatic symptoms and past illnesses; the second, with psychological symptoms. Each "yes" response means that the patient has a particular symptom. Too many yeses, then—particularly on psychiatrically significant items—would suggest an underlying emotional disorder.[4]

THE PATIENT "PROJECTS" ANXIETY

Informative as the questionnaires frequently are, too often the patient may try to give the answers he thinks are "wanted," and thus may alter the true picture. With the "projective" tests, on the other hand, there clearly are no right or wrong answers. The subject simply describes what he "sees" in an ink blot, builds up a story around the characters in a picture, or draws a picture of a person or object. Because he is not sure what the examiner is looking for, and because he can rarely help "projecting" his own problems into an ambiguous situation, his responses are believed to be far more revealing than answers he might give to specific questions, oral or written.

Best known of the projective tests is, of course, the Rorschach Ink Blot Test, named for its designer and first published in Switzerland in 1921. (Rorschach was not the first to use ink blots for personality studies; other psychologists had used them, including Binet and Henri in 1895.) The test consists of 10 cards, on each of which is one bisymmetric ink blot, some in color. The subject's response

Fig. 36. Example of Rorschach Ink Blot Test Card.

to each is examined with a number of questions in mind: "Where on the blot was the response object seen?" (Location.) "What was seen?" (Content.) "What characteristic of the blot suggested the response or why was it seen?" (Determinant.) "How well did the response correspond to the contour of the blot area?" (Form-Level.) "How commonly is this response given by other persons?" (Originality.) [5]

Both the subject's characteristic way of responding to the blots as well as the kind of objects he sees determine the final interpretation of his personality. Although scoring the Rorschach is not too difficult, *interpreting* the scores requires a good deal of skill, training and experience, and usually requires a psychologist or psychiatrist.

Some of the Rorschach responses that have been considered signs of anxiety [6]:

Disgusting (to the patient) material. "*A furry spider (in inquiry expressed disgust); a dirty color; a splotch of mud, looks dirty; looks like a slimy reptile.*"

Figures that are directly threatening or fearful. "*. . . looks like the face of a devil or something, some monster face with pink ears. Devils, with a fire burning; . . . this is full of shadows in here, I can't make out what it might be. Something fearful; huge bird clutching in toward this figure of a man here.*"

Figures suggestive of anxiety or usually deemed phobic in nature. "*Clouds, shadows, x-rays, parts of bodies such as eyes, pointing fingers . . . a giant ray; a gorilla; smoke, like from a fire . . . Fish with dorsal fin spread out as if in flight; an animal running away from something; . . . a rat, long tail; a pointing hand.*"

Evasive answers. *Vague maps or "splotches."—"A map; like red ink spilt; a diagram of something.*"

Rejection of the card altogether.

Responses emphasizing gloom or sadness. "*This looks dull or lifeless, like a dead leaf; eroded soil, barren and sterile; a dead branch. An iceberg.*"

Lack of balance, or instability, verbalized as part of a response. "*This looks like two animals balanced precariously on a rock; this looks like a man climbing a mountain, he is reaching across to someone else, he seems to be slipping. . . .*"

Confusion or indecision verbalized as part of the response. "*A group of insects milling about not knowing what to do; the whole thing represents confusion to me . . .*"

Confusion over the sex of a figure. "*I can't make this out, can be either men or women; two figures ? I can't tell, highheeled shoes, yet they have male dress. This looks like breasts. . . .*"

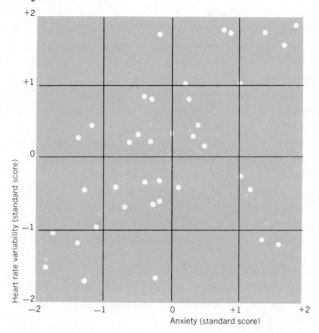

Fig. 37. "Scatter plot" of patient's heart rate and anxiety. Correlation between a patient's heart rate variability and his anxiety as rated by psychiatrists is shown by this "scatter plot." The physiologic and psychological measurements are reduced to "standard scores," in which the mean is taken to be zero and the deviation from the mean is independent of the raw scores. When the observations are plotted, their elliptical pattern indicates that the variables correlate positively but moderately.—*Adapted from* R. B. Cattell.[8]

FACTOR ANALYSIS OF ANXIETY

While most of these well-known psychological tests are designed to measure many other factors besides anxiety, Raymond B. Cattell and his colleagues at the University of Illinois have for years been taking a more direct approach. The reason is simple. "Until we can define and measure it," the psychologist has said, "the emergence and testing of any laws or theories about causes and consequences of anxiety is the merest of vanity." [7] In their laboratory at the University, Cattell and his co-workers have been applying a mathematicostatistical method called Factor Analysis to the problem of defining and measuring anxiety. This method "measures many specific manifestations in the field concerned and finds out what goes with what. . . ."

During their 10-year experimental period, the investigators have made a "correlational examination" of more than 400 alleged manifestations of anxiety, including such things as high heart rate, poor hand-steadiness, inability to look someone in the eye, dry mouth, sinking feeling in the stomach, and so on. Many of these variables have turned out to be positive and significant indicators of anxiety, but some have not (see Fig. 37).

Results of objective tests were found to correlate with the results of certain anxiety questionnaires. Both discriminated well between anxious and nonanxious individuals. Eventually, therefore, the psychologists developed an objective test battery—which they called the objective-analytic (O-A) battery—and a short 40-item questionnaire that could be more easily used by the general physician. Their various studies, Cattell noted, definitely pointed "to the existence of a single, pervasive factor of anxiety." However, several factors with high anxiety content were also discovered, and Cattell suggested that there may be "a common reservoir of anxiety to which ego weakness, guilt proneness, frustrated drive, and other primary factors contribute. . . ." [8]

Anxiety Further Defined

The Illinois psychologists have also been able to distinguish anxiety from similar states with which it is often confused. The

TABLE 8. *Average tested anxiety levels in 24 occupational groups*

ANXIETY/PERCENTILE	GROUP
Relatively higher 60th to 80th	Editorial workers (publishing house office); science fiction writers; US Navy underwater demolition team; USAF pilot cadets in training; artists; farmers; general writers
Middle ranges 40th to 60th	Executives (business, managerial); elementary school teachers; sales managers; Catholic priests; Olympic athletes; cooks (kitchen help, female); retail salesmen; wholesale salesmen; nurses (female); city police; undergraduate college students; psychiatric technicians; medical school students
Relatively lower 20th to 40th	Researchers (physics, biology, psychology); clerks (female, filing and typing); aircraft engineering apprentices (no college degree); university administrators

anxiety pattern, they note, differs somewhat from the effort-stress pattern (effort-stress shows no anxiety or emotionality, only strong concentration and perhaps awareness of effort); it differs from the fear pattern (among other differences, anxiety produces increased salivation and gastric secretion); and it differs from the neurosis pattern as well (neurotics differ from normal individuals in at least six personality factors, of which anxiety is one). The more precise measurements of anxiety now possible have demonstrated significant differences in anxiety levels with age, occupation (see Table 8), national cultures and—most important, of course—with clinical syndromes (see Table 9).

TABLE 9. *Average tested anxiety levels of 20 groups of clinical interest as compared to normals* [9]

PERCENTILE *	GROUP/STATE
90th	Anxiety reaction or state
85th	Depression, depressive reaction; neurotics generally; male homosexuals
80th	Male sociopaths; narcotics users; alcoholics
75th	Inadequate personality; psychopaths; obsessive-compulsive neurosis
70th	Conversion reaction; deafness or serious hearing disability
65th	Male convicts; physical disability interfering with locomotion; schizophrenic psychosis
60th	Disabled male veterans; psychotics generally
55th	Blindness or serious visual disability; manic-depressive psychosis
50th	Normal or unselected adults; male psychosomatic disorders

* Any of the values of a variable which separate the entire distribution into 100 groups of equal frequency

What does the future hold? The time may come when such improved and standardized tests may not only provide differential diagnoses to the various emotional states associated with anxiety, but, by accurately determining the patient's level of anxiety, also indicate the specific therapy required.

CHAPTER 19 BIBLIOGRAPHY

1. Freeman, F. S.: Theory and Practice of Psychological Testing, ed 3, New York, Holt, Rinehart and Winston, Inc., 1962.
2. Taylor, J. A.: J Abnorm Soc Psychol *48*:285, 1953.
3. Swenson, W. M., and Pearson, J. S.: Meth Inform Med *3*:34, 1964.
4. Brown, A. C., and Fry, J.: J Psychosom Res *6*:185, 1962.
5. Ulett, G. A., and Goodrich, D. W.: A Synopsis of Contemporary Psychiatry, ed 2, St. Louis, Mosby, 1960.
6. De Vos, G.: J Project Techn *16*:133, 1952.
7. Medical News: JAMA *188*:(3)49, 1964.
8. Cattell, R. B.: Sci Amer *208*:96, 1963.
9. Scheier, I. H.: Ann NY Acad Sci *93*:840, 1962.

INDEX

2849

Library
I.U.P.
Indiana, PA